The PRINCIPAL'S Essential Guide to LITERACY in the ELEMENTARY SCHOOL

Autumn Tooms, Nancy Padak, and Timothy Rasinski

Foreword by Gay Fawcett

 **SCHOLASTIC**

New York • Toronto • London • Auckland • Sydney
Mexico City • New Delhi • Hong Kong • Buenos Aires

Editor: Sarah Glasscock
Cover designer and illustration: Jay Namerow
Interior designer: Maria Lilja
Photo credits ©: Photos.com (page 12), Maria Lilja (page 36), Digital Vision/Getty Images (page 58), Comstock (page 76), Image 100 via SODA (page 100), Photos.com (page 118), Greg Vote/V Stock LLC/ Index Open (page 140), Corbis Photography/Veer (page 174), Index Open (page 190)

ISBN 13: 978-0-439-70484-7 • ISBN 10: 0-439-70484-7

Table of Contents

Acknowledgements

We wish to acknowledge the many principals, teachers, and parents who have celebrated children's reading achievements and supported classroom efforts toward excellence. Autumn wishes to specifically mention her favorite reading teacher, Georgia Tooms, who in 1962 taught first-grade English Language Learners to read at the Second Mesa Day School, near the village of Shungopavi, on the Hopi Indian reservation, years before she taught her own daughter to read.

—A, N, T

Foreword by Gay Fawcett

Recently an elementary principal was in the news because the students in his building had met his challenge of reading 10,000 books. He had bargained with them; if they read 10,000 books, they could choose their reward. The reward they chose was to send him to the roof of the school at bedtime. He later commented that he knew it would be cold but he had no idea *how* cold it would be. It was December—in New York!

These stories are fairly common. Principals kiss pigs, take a pie in the face, and shave their heads—just to get students to read. I certainly understand and have great empathy for them. When I was a principal, there were many times I would have done just about anything (short of shaving my head!) to get Brandi, A. J., Kimmie, and Cody to read books. Principals know with certainty that independent reading improves reading achievement, and so in desperation they try crazy things to lure kids to books. The good news is, there is an alternative. Tooms, Padak, and Rasinski show the way in this book.

There is no question about it—principals can make a difference in student achievement. Effective schools research in the 1970s and early 1980s pointed to strong instructional leadership as a correlate to student learning. More recent studies affirm that principal leadership can have a dramatic effect on student achievement (see, for example, Marzano, 2003). But it doesn't just happen. It takes skill and expertise to be a literacy leader. This book provides principals with the information they need about how young children learn to read as well as practical suggestions for how to establish a culture of literacy among students, staff, parents, and community.

What I like most about *The Principal's Essential Guide to Literacy in the Elementary School* is that it begins by helping principals to get in touch with their own literacy values. Too often professional books attempt to *convince* us of what we should believe. Tooms, Padak, and Rasinski instead ask principals to examine their own beliefs about literacy so that they can lead with clear principles and conviction. However, rather than presenting a series of philosophical questions, the authors ask questions that cause principals to reflect on themselves as literate people. The reader goes away with a distinct understanding of literate behavior; you can't give it to someone else if you don't have it yourself!

The book moves principals through a logical sequence of assessing the school's literacy culture, establishing school-wide goals, and developing an action plan that includes staff, students, parents, and community. Amazingly, all this is done through simple strategies that will provide profound results. Principals will appreciate that the suggestions require little preparation time but have big payoffs.

At the same time, the authors do support their assertions and suggestions with research. However, their keen sense of the busy principal-reader keeps them from belaboring the research. They move from meeting strategies, like "hot dottings," to hot topics such as scientifically based reading research without missing a beat.

I could relate to the stories real principals told throughout the book. I know people just like the motorcycle custodian, Randy. Regrettably, I have been a participant in the Abilene Paradox, and, like Susan, I have attended staff development sessions that I nearly didn't make it through. The stories about all these principals reminded me that we are not alone in this role. There are others who have wrestled with the same kinds of problems and celebrated the same kinds of successes, and by turning to one another, we can become better leaders in this often lonely position.

A real strength of the book is that you don't have to read it straight through. You can decide which chapter is most relevant for you right now and start there. If in perusing the Table of Contents nothing jumps out at you, I would recommend you go directly to the month-by-month staff development calendar in Chapter 7 for suggestions that will provoke conversation and invoke growth among your teachers.

If after reading *The Principal's Essential Guide to Literacy in the Elementary School*, you still want to go to the roof, no doubt you will capture the attention of some hard-core reluctant readers, so go on up. Just two pieces of advice as you head to the ladder: don't go in December, and take this book with you for your bedtime reading.

Reference: Marzano, R.J. (2003). *What works in schools: Translating research into action*. Alexandria, VA: Association for Supervision and Curriculum Development.

Introduction

Have you ever had to suffer through one of those staff development *things*? You know what we're talking about: the luncheons and the weekend "institutes" that sound great on paper but are filled with pedantic experts who never really answer the question that it took you ten minutes to get up the courage to ask. Yes, we've been to those things, too, and we've seen our friends, the principals, humbly retreat from the patronizing answers thrown at them and completely disengage from the topic.

We wrote this book because we're weary of the abyss between the principal who's trying to do it all and the mountain of research on literacy that demands endless attention and consideration. We three authors actually became friends because we each understand the reality of working in schools. Autumn Tooms is a former principal. Nancy Padak is a former reading specialist and district office curriculum administrator. Tim Rasinski is a former reading specialist. All three of us are now professors who teach, think, and write about issues in our respective fields.

Although we're not in the same program at our university, our friendship developed through a series of hallway conversations about the true joy of working with children and the hellish nature of navigating through the rigors and pitfalls of instructional leadership in the public school system. We learned through our brief exchanges at the copy machine or in the mailroom that we share a commitment to translating research into plain language for educators who are in the classroom.

Like most teachers, all three of us have a soft spot for children's literature. At the moment we decided to really embark on this writing adventure, it was Nancy who said, "Go dog, go!" And when Autumn spied *Charlotte's*

Web on a shelf in Tim's infamously messy office, he waded through the many piles of books and papers to retrieve the book and present it to her. It took three years of conversations to realize that we had something significant to say about literacy, not only to each other but also to principals and teachers who are trying, like us, to help children unlock the magic that is embedded in acquired reading skills. Our hope is that you find the information in the following pages relevant, easy to digest, and, above all, helpful.

CHAPTER 1

Why Is Leadership in Literacy Important?

T he first thing that we want you, our reader, to consider is that a principal's career development is a process that takes place within two contradictory realities that make up what we call "the Paradox of Educational Authority." Although this descriptor sounds terribly academic, it's really not that difficult to understand. The first reality is centered on a universal notion that principals are expected to be omniscient simply because they're the leaders of their schools. Leading a school requires a multitude of diverse responsibilities, including student discipline, public relations, instruction, construction and site maintenance, therapy for teachers and parents, as well as lunchtime loan officer and taxi driver. Stakeholders, from the janitor to the president of the parent–teacher organization, expect their principal to be the one person on campus who knows everything about the school—and everything related to the field of education.

The second reality, which is in direct conflict to the first, is that principals have so much to do that they can't possibly be as omniscient as stakeholders expect them to be. Principals often have a somewhat narrow knowledge base in terms of curriculum because as teachers they specialized in one area. Furthermore, to attain principal licensure, most states require a graduate course of study focused on organizational management and leadership and not on curriculum and instruction. Thus, a principal feels pressure from different groups to know everything, and yet, because of background and training, he or she can't possibly meet their demands. No one could. However, rather than jilting the stakeholders in our community, we often feel forced to do something in order to maintain the aura of being in charge: we maintain our position as leader by faking it. This isn't bad; in fact, it's a necessary skill. In most cases, faking it doesn't imply lying. It is the art of schmoozing, of saying, "What you're asking is important enough to deserve a response; I'll get back to you." Yet sometimes that doesn't happen because we simply don't have the time to ferret out the answers to the problems. Sometimes faking it means that we speak only in the most superficial ways about what's happening in terms of teaching and learning because we don't have real depth to our knowledge base.

The Paradox of Educational Authority is illustrated beautifully by the former basketball coach, now the principal of a high school, charged with facilitating the development of a new instructional vision for the school. Or the former high school biology teacher, now the principal of a middle school, mired in trying to implement a new school-within-a-school model with her staff. Another example is the dynamic and beloved former middle school social studies teacher, now the principal of a K-5 school in academic emergency. All three of these leaders have earned reputations as strong, effective professionals in their classrooms and community. Ironically, these admirable strengths have helped them to ascend to positions that require them to make decisions about teaching and learning in areas where they have little or no experience and training.

Principals new to the position usually take two or three years just to get comfortable with the rhythms of their role and the demands of the school year. Any effort a principal makes toward his or her own professional development is usually driven by pressure from the state or governing board. For example, a principal may want to learn about the new math or reading program but instead has to invest time in decoding standardized test scores because there is not enough time to explore both areas. They must compensate by delegating tasks that are more central to classroom professional development or instructional assistance to assistant principals or curriculum specialists. The problem is that these leadership team members are usually not responsible for evaluating classroom teachers. Therefore, teachers may perceive a gap between their evaluation process, which "counts" because the principal conducts it, and professional development activities conducted by someone who doesn't evaluate them. This gap can widen when the principal doesn't choose to weave the outcomes from professional development into the evaluation process. In other words, why should a teacher worry about the amount of time spent in class on sentence strips, which was the focus of last week's in-service, if the principal doesn't mention expectations for this in a pre-observation conference?

All of these factors ultimately contribute to what is at the heart of the paradox: The person who has the most authority and power to hold teachers accountable is often the person least confident to do so because he or she hasn't been able to invest the time to learn the specifics about what a particular reading, math, or science lesson should look like. Do you need an example to refresh your memory? Think about the time when you really wanted to question a teacher on the specifics of a lesson you observed but felt reluctant to do so because of the difficulty in expressing your concerns. You didn't want to argue with the teacher because he was trained in, say, Reading Recovery, and you weren't. While the teacher flashed sentence strips and gave the impression that he knew it all in the classroom, you were wondering if it was acceptable not to explore digraphs and word families during the lesson.

Sometimes, curriculum directors and superintendents understand this technical problem and attempt to address it by structuring in-services and training for their principals. However, these sorts of workshops are often ineffective as management issues easily distract administrators. Ultimately, principals don't like to admit it when they have a shallow contextual framework in a particular area of instruction. If they did so, they would have to relinquish that aura of omniscience that was granted to them with the job title. The unspoken truth about curriculum leadership among principals is that when you admit you don't know something, you lose credibility as the leader. Obviously, for most principals, this is most dangerous territory.

So then how does the old basketball coach who's the new principal figure out what a good lesson looks like when she's conducting an observation in a third-grade classroom? That's the primary question and driving force behind this book. Our efforts in the following pages are meant to help principals, and the people who work with them, recognize the nuts and bolts of the single most important area of learning that takes place in a school: literacy.

Why is literacy so important?

The reason literacy should be the highest priority above all other lines of instruction is simple: one needs to read to be able to function at the most basic level in society. Employment with a decent wage, success in school, satisfaction in daily life, and the ability to stay connected to one's community are all predicated on the ability to read. However, the concept of literacy involves more than the process of understanding the words on a page or a computer screen. According to Rubin (1986):

> Literacy is not a quality that one possesses or doesn't possess.
> It is not like red hair and freckles, permanently distinguishing
> some people. Nor is reading like having a healthy heart muscle

that one builds up and maintains through practice. Rather, reading is something one does. Literacy, likewise, is a way of coming in contact with the world. Some people engage in literate behavior with greater frequency and intensity than others. Some people use literate behavior to expand their worlds across time and space. Some people read traffic signs and cereal boxes. (p. 7)

As stated before, we understand the tension that exists between the demand for principals to be omniscient and the complete lack of time they have to be an expert in all areas of schooling. However, we believe leadership in literacy is crucial to a school's success and should be grounded in the answers to the following questions:

  ＊ How do you determine your own values about literacy and empower others to do the same?

  ＊ How do you assess the literacy values in your school?

  ＊ What happens when groups have different values about literacy?

  ＊ How do you build a culture of literacy in your school?

  ＊ How do you lead literacy instruction?

  ＊ Why is a literacy committee important, and who should be on it?

In this chapter, we'll look at each of these questions and the implications of their answers.

How do you determine your values about literacy and empower others to do the same?

The first step to helping your school community value literacy is to look inward and reflect on your own literary habits. Consider the value of doing this chronologically. In other words, go back and remember what it was like to be in first grade. How did you learn to read? Did you suffer through the Dick and Jane series, or did you look forward to their adventures? Can you remember if your teacher had a reading chart on the wall with your name on it? Did you get a gold star for every book you read? Perhaps you remember the drills the teacher conducted by pointing at different members of word families written on the chalkboard. Do you remember reciting "sad, bad, mad, dad" with the rest of your classmates? Perhaps you were in a reading group. Did you like having to read out loud?

Now consider what reading was like in your home. Can you remember your parents reading to you? Can you remember anyone reading to you? Did anyone in your family read for pleasure? Was your home filled with magazines and newspapers or books? Were they in English or another language? Did your mother read the newspaper every morning at the table or perhaps read something she enjoyed only on the weekends?

Switch gears again and consider your own current literacy habits. When and in what context do you read? Is it while you're on the treadmill, at dinner, or on the couch on a lazy Sunday? What motivates you to read? Some people read when they're at home on a snowy day, and some people read when they get stuck in traffic. Any of these motivators is perfectly acceptable. Also, think about when you enjoy reading and how it might be related to the various activities of your day such as mealtime, unwinding from the day, or relaxing on a weekend. Do you tend to buy a new book when you hear about it on television or read about it in the newspaper? How long is the time between when you buy a book and actually read it?

What is significant about these habits is that they were probably acquired gradually and subconsciously.

Reflecting on how you became literate and what inspires you to read will help you be conscious of the different ways that literate behavior has become part of your life. Once you've completed this personal reflection, write down the answers to the questions in the three previous paragraphs and look for patterns in your answers.

All of the above questions can be used as a framework for a discussion about literate behavior with your staff and community. Begin this exercise by placing the group of people you're working with into groups of four to six people. Supply each group with a large tablet of chart paper. Ask the groups to brainstorm answers to the questions and list them in different categories. For example, the first category might be their reflections on the experience of learning to read. The second might be what they remember reading as they were growing up. The next category might be what they read as adults. The final category might be when each group member reads. (You may add or change as many categories as you like; these are suggestions to get you started.)

Next, have the groups reconvene into a large group and give each person three red adhesive dots. These adhesive dots are available in multiple colors in the label section at any office supply store. Invite your audience to walk around the room and review the information on the charts. Assign everyone the task of giving the most value to three items on the chart. Thus, they're invited to put a red dot next to the item that's most important to them, and because they only have three dots, they can only mark the three items they find most important.

After your audience has prioritized the lists, reconvene as a large group and find the items with the greatest number of red dots. List them on chart paper to see which items the group values the most. This "hot dot" exercise is a quick method to empower a group of people to determine their values about topics ranging from literacy to playground equipment.

While you're assessing literacy values, keep in mind that there is a wide range of literate behavior ranging from intense to effortless and each type of reading has its place. The key is variety and the choice to engage in different levels of activity. Anna Quindlen (1998) likened reading to a buffet. Some reading material, like Tolstoy's *War and Peace* is without question roast beef. Novels, like those written by John Grisham, are super-sized combo meals. Then there are juicy side dishes such as the articles in *The New Yorker* magazine or the little gift books displayed beside the cash register at the bookstore. Poetry, jokes, interesting words, and inspirational quotes are appetizers and dessert. The buffet analogy provides another opportunity for your faculty and community to "hot dotting." Ask them to list what kinds of material they read, along with what motivates them to read it. For instance, do they read because the book is assigned in a graduate class or because they read about an article on the Internet? These exercises not only help your staff to think about what they value about reading, but they also start your faculty focusing on more systemic questions about your school and literacy values.

How do you assess the literacy values in your school?

These "hot dotting" exercises can form the core of a two-day workshop, a two-hour staff meeting, or a series of community meetings. The length of time you invest in this activity depends on your preference; however, you should conduct them in two phases.

In the first phase, which was discussed in the previous section, participants reflect on 1) how they became literate and 2) their current literate behaviors and values. By modeling the "hot dotting" exercise in a faculty meeting, you are both empowering and inviting your teachers to repeat this activity with their students in class. Allow time for grade-level teachers to meet and "hot dot" the three most important items that their students selected. Finally, bring your faculty together to compare what teachers value related to their own literate behavior and their discoveries about what their students valued. Gather the perspectives of community members to add a third perspective to your analysis of literacy values. When comparing all three constituencies, your staff should be able to see trends and gaps in values. The trends and gaps are what form the foundation of a vision you and your staff can create concerning the culture of literate behavior at your school.

The second phase of this activity focuses on asking the student population, the faculty, and the community to reflect on what could be done to improve students' literate behavior. Consider including the following subcategories: what attitudes could and should be modeled for students (and by whom), what resources are available, and what collaborations are possible. Use the same "hot dotting" technique to have groups brainstorm and prioritize ideas for improvement, assessment, parental involvement, summer reading programs, favorite reading genre, and so on.

What happens when groups have different values about literacy?

A common challenge associated with "hot dotting" is that one constituency may have a great idea that another group doesn't support. This gives the principal the opportunity to use his or her facilitation and leadership skills. Holly LaVerne, a principal in Killeen, Texas, shares her story to illustrate this conundrum:

> I had been a principal for two years in a K-8 school of twelve hundred students. Our community was working on making our school the focus of some extended neighborhood activities. Someone had the great idea of having a weekly pajama reading party for the students. Basically we would invite families to come to school from 7:00 to 9:00 in the evening and read books with teachers in the library. We would invite kids to wear their pajamas and bring a favorite teddy bear or a pillow. Everyone was real excited about it until the teachers got wind of the idea. When I had asked for volunteers from the teaching staff, many of the

faculty voiced a concern that they should be paid to participate in this event because it was after contracted hours. Within a week I had gone from ten committed volunteers to about three "maybe" volunteers. So I decided to have a series of three faculty meetings to talk about our literacy goals as a school.

For the first meeting, I asked the faculty to bring their standardized test scores with them to discuss. After we reviewed the scores, we talked about where improvements could be made. While we all agreed that everyone was working hard—we did see that we could make other efforts to focus on giving our students more practice with their reading skills. After a great deal of discussion we also reached an agreement that reading was the key to raising the scores.

The second meeting with the faculty was spent brainstorming a list of activities we could do in the classroom and throughout the school day to put a focus on reading. This was not the easiest discussion. We had to accept that some things we were doing were not working and we had to look at why. One of the things we learned was that our Drop Everything And Read (DEAR) time was no longer 45 minutes in the school day. It was now 20 minutes, and I had the uncomfortable task of reminding teachers that they needed to read along with the students as well as make sure the students were really reading. Grading papers was not appropriate during DEAR time. Neither was allowing students to nap. I also realized I had to make a greater effort to sweep through all the classrooms during DEAR time on a regular basis so my faculty understood that I took this effort seriously. The first month after the meeting, I made a point to consistently get into those classrooms during DEAR time and after a while teachers were doing what I had hoped. I started writing thank-you notes for their extra efforts and making a point of recognizing their efforts in the hallway.

By the time the third meeting with the faculty arrived, we were ready to talk about the importance of valuing reading as a school community. I had to help the teachers get past the finger pointing at parents. Yes, parents are ultimately responsible for their kids, but teachers can't keep using that as an excuse. So we decided to talk about what it meant to embrace accountability. I used my own reflections as to what happened with DEAR time once we all decided to focus on really reading as a school. I invited teachers to share stories of what they had seen in their students in terms of reading in the last two months.

After we shared some challenges and successes we went back and talked about pajama night. I had purposely let this issue go in the last two months because I wanted instead to focus on helping the faculty see how important reading was. Then we discussed it. I offered up an idea that would only require two teachers a month to supervise during pajama night for the entire school year. Then a teacher's aide even volunteered to help. So in the end we were able to have our pajama party reading program. And more teachers were willing to volunteer without being paid because the inconvenience was only two evenings in one month for the entire school year. The process took almost an entire semester to get buy-in from the teachers, and we had to wait another semester to start the program, but in the end we did it. And I would rather have taken a longer time to get everyone behind a program than to hurry up and do something in a half-hearted way with minimal support from the staff. I think the key in the end was that the staff finally understood why this was important and that because the responsibilities were divided equally among faculty, the inconvenience was at a minimum for people. Plus, once we started the parties, people found out they were fun; we even had the local grocery store donate graham crackers and apples for bedtime snacks.

Holly's story is a cogent example of why timing and tenacity are such integral pieces of leadership. Groups within an organization typically consist of a spectrum of people who buy into change with varying levels of enthusiasms. Some can see immediately the benefits of a change and have no problem switching gears. Conversely, there are usually a similar number of people who have no intention of changing their daily work efforts. The majority of group members lie in between these two extremes. This middle faction requires the most attention and effort from the principal. They need to hear (often more than once) the challenges and expectations expressed in realistic terms. Furthermore, helping a staff accept a new set of responsibilities is a task that requires multiple efforts to get the message across. Because Holly was willing to take the time to let her staff share their concerns through a series of meetings, as well as consistently set expectations, she experienced some success. Finally, we think it's noteworthy that Holly realized the importance of changing her own behavior (i.e., increasing the amount of time she spent in classrooms) so that her staff viewed her concerns and vision as credible.

How do you build a culture of literacy in your school?

In order to address this question, first think about what a "culture of literacy" is. A school's culture is something that is palpable to any campus visitor. It's the sum of the actions of the school's members in conjunction with the symbols displayed on everything from stationery to the school marquee to hallway signs. This conjunction of actions and symbols is what truly defines a school's culture. Without these two factors working in tandem, you find a school that may have a great slogan like *all children can learn* that's, in reality, hollow and sterile because, in truth, its teachers aren't focused on individualized instruction. Whatever slogan or symbol a school adopts must be lived in its day-to-day operation and in every facet of its community. Ensuring that the symbol or slogan is a living part of all facets of a school community (and therefore, truly representative of a culture) is where the job of the principal lies.

Building a school culture starts with assessing *what is, and what is not, valued by the many different constituencies of your school community.* In order to do this, first consider how you can use the same results from the "hot dotting" activities with your faculty to support your evaluation of instruction in terms of the strengths and weaknesses in your classrooms. For example, if you find that your community and your teachers have said that reading is important, use this as a lens to review teachers' lesson plans. Do you see provisions in the plans for students to read in class or during the learning day? Do you see provisions for students to build their vocabulary during class? Are there blocks of time designated for students to read to each other? How is the school librarian involved with lessons?

When you look at what's happening in the classroom, remember also to consider the difference between what a teacher puts in a lesson plan and what actually happens every day in a classroom. Regular, unannounced visits to a class not only increase your visibility but also allow you to see what students are learning during the school day.

Unfortunately, classroom visits may be on the top of a principal's list of priorities, but a visit is often the first thing to be eliminated from a principal's schedule because of all the fires that must be put out first. That's because one of the hardest things for principals to do is to set boundaries with their time. For instance, there's often someone in the administrative office lodging a complaint or a student who needs to be disciplined. These problems usually take longer than anticipated, and principals end up sacrificing time allotted to visiting a classroom, particularly if the visit isn't a formal observation.

If this is happening to you, stop this behavior. Learn to set boundaries and to tell people that you have another appointment—because you do. Being in the classroom and observing and participating in the teaching and learning process is the most important thing a principal does. And when a principal fails to be involved in the teaching and learning within a school, he or she loses credibility with the staff and ultimately the community.

You can avoid this irreparable circumstance. When your school is out of session in July and you have time alone to think without distraction, schedule three twenty-minute pop-in classroom visits per teacher, per grading period, in your calendar. Schedule these pop-ins so that every teacher is seen regularly on an informal basis in addition to his or her formal observations. You can code formal visits with blue ink and pop-ins with red ink. That way, you understand the difference, but to your secretary or anyone else who looks at your calendar, you have appointments documented that take precedence over seeming emergencies. By inserting the pop-ins on your calendar, you are committing the time to visiting classrooms that would otherwise be eaten up by the day-to-day demands of your job. It is much easier for your secretary to tell an angry parent that you have a meeting in someone's classroom if it is written on your calendar. Also, if your secretary doesn't know that you are keeping time for classroom visits sacred, then she or he is more likely to call you away from this valuable time in order to solve a problem immediately. You'll find that many of these problems can actually wait when you have committed on your calendar to visiting classrooms.

It's very important to remember to adhere consistently to your scheduled visits. It's not necessary (or wise) to inform your teachers ahead of time that you're popping in for a visit. Remember, pop-ins are scheduled in your calendar so that your secretary (and you) remember that you are not to be called away from your time in a classroom unless there is a real emergency. Scheduling pop-ins also lets you plan your day more efficiently so that you dedicate time to visiting classrooms when literacy instruction is happening rather than just whenever you can squeeze in the time.

The element of surprise will help teachers and students become more comfortable with your presence during a lesson, and you'll have a better chance to see what's really happening in class. If you sacrifice consistency where these visits are concerned, you ultimately sacrifice involvement with the teaching and learning process and with holding people accountable.

Another helpful strategy is to train your secretary to understand that nothing except immediate danger to students interrupts your visits to classrooms. Also help your secretary understand the importance of bringing meetings to closure by having her interrupt the meeting you might be in to announce that you have another meeting to attend. If you let one meeting run ten minutes over at the beginning of the day, that ten minutes can grow by leaps and bounds by lunch. No one appreciates lateness, and being the boss is no excuse. Principals often think they're allowed to be late simply because they have so many places to be within a school community.

Phillip Pizzatola, a teacher in Kent, Ohio, reflects on how his principal's lateness affected his relationship with the staff and his credibility:

> You know he was always late. And we all knew it was because he let someone corner him for a chat after a meeting. So the first meeting ran over into the second and so on. We would end up waiting for him over 20 minutes, every time, and he would enter the room and look at each one of us and say, "I owe each one of you ten minutes for being late." That meant nothing to us because he was late every time. Our time was valuable and he had no respect for it. His "I owe you ten minutes" excuses were the beginning of the end for him. Pretty soon he was asking for us to help him with stuff and no one wanted to go the extra mile for him and his ideas because we didn't respect him.

Once you feel confident about *what is* on your campus through "hot dotting" and consistent visits to classrooms, the next phase of building a culture of literacy is to look for the gaps between *what is*, *what the stakeholders believe reality is*, and *what could and should be*. Find uninterrupted time to concentrate and make a series of lists that reflect each of these categories. Then prioritize them yourself using the "hot dotting" method. Next, invite your leadership team to do the same. Use this process to discuss the realities that center on challenges related to personnel and resources. The result of this process is the framework for your school's vision for a literacy culture.

The parts of a literacy culture can be divided into the following:

A. what happens in the classroom that's related to literacy

B. what happens during the school day, outside the classroom, that's related to literacy

C. what happens outside the school day, at school, that's related to literacy in the community

D. what happens outside the school day, off campus, that's related to literacy in the community

The most obvious part of a literacy culture is item A, what happens in the classroom that's related to literacy. In this arena, the focus is on more than reading programs; it also encompasses what your faculty is doing in tandem to focus on reading. For example, ask yourself if you really understand your school's reading program. Have you, as the principal, been to training sessions for the program, or do you depend completely on your reading specialist to know all the ins and outs of it? Secondly, how is the reading program related to your teacher evaluations and faculty professional development activities? It's most important that you provide some sort of bridge between staff development and accountability in literacy. If you don't, your staff will be less motivated to really utilize the training they receive in a particular literacy program.

Another item related to literacy and staff development is the effort you make to keep your staff updated on current ideas about reading and literacy. Do you have a staff subscription to literacy journals such as *The Reading Teacher*? Are the journals in a staff professional-development library in the teachers' lounge? Does your school have a professional book subscription to the International Reading Association? Do you have regular book talks or article reviews with your staff to go over certain articles? Moreover, do you make time to read them yourself and discuss them with colleagues?

In terms of what happens outside the classroom for students, what collaborations do you encourage with your staff? Is there DEAR (Drop Everything And Read) time at your school? Do you encourage your teachers to regularly engage in shared reading programs between grade levels? Do you have grade-level or school-wide poetry contests? Do you, the principal, make visits to classes to read a chapter or a poem to students on a regular basis? Do you have a system in place that asks parents to volunteer to be guest readers? If not parents, what about enlisting the help of staff members who are not teachers to visit classrooms and read once a week? Students can be inspired by people you might not think of right away. Allison Jayce, a principal in Scottsdale, Arizona, recalls this story about using other staff members to read to students:

> Rick was our school's head custodian. He had long blond hair in a ponytail, drove a motorcycle, and wore a goatee. He was just the epitome of cool and he lived in the neighborhood. Every kid knew him and every kid adored him. He was the cross between Clint Eastwood and a pirate. He was pretty quiet and didn't say much to the kids but they loved it that he had this Harley motorcycle and wore a leather jacket. We were trying to figure out how to get the kids to understand that reading was a cool thing. So when we started doing guest readers in classes, I asked Rick if he would be willing to read a poem or a story of his choosing to the kids near the end of lunch recess. And then whoever wanted to listen could. I even told him he could pick a grade and the place to read it. He picked fifth and he asked if he could read it on top of the roof of the cafeteria. So he agreed to read poems from *Where the Sidewalk Ends* by Shel Silverstein. He was a little nervous and you could tell he felt silly doing this—but I tell you, he was the talk of the campus for at least a month. We had put up signs that said where to meet Rick and then he and an aide helped about ten kids go through the back of the cafeteria and up through the fire escape ladder to the top of the roof to hear the reading. It was like the kids were let in on a secret with the trip up to the roof. They loved it. Then the word spread. So Rick did it again, only this time he led them to the back of the workshop and read another poem. Then he parked his motorcycle on the stage, read from the seat and then drove the thing

across the stage. The kids went nuts. They loved it! We had an aide supervise the stage so the kids paid attention while Rick was reading. He was so popular, the teachers ended up delivering thank-you letters to him for reading. We ended up calling this thing "adventures at Rick's café," and we held it once a month. At first he was reticent because he needed to get his custodial work done—but he really had rock star status with our kids. So he read to the kids, the cafeteria took a little longer to clean on Fridays, and I heard from a parent that there was a run on Shel Silverstein's books at the local bookstore. Now I have him reading to our kindergartners and they love him too. He will park that bike on the stage, turn off the engine and pick someone from the audience to sit on the bike seat with him while he is reading. He has loosened up a little around our younger kids, and the staff can't get over how cool reading has now become in the eyes of our students.

Modeling a commitment to professional development is essential to maintaining a cultural value of anything. Once your subordinates realize that something is important to you, then they'll tend to embrace that value because they know they're likely to be held accountable for it. Just as you scheduled in your planner time to pop in to classrooms, make a date to engage in professional reading once a week. A good way to do this is to schedule lunch out of the building for yourself and to bring some reading material. Most principals open up their buildings long before their staff arrives and leave with the night custodians. Therefore, taking a break in the middle of the day is not only perfectly ethical, it will help save your sanity. You may want to catch some reading time in your office with the door closed. Be advised, however, that the odds are that you'll be interrupted and won't be able to concentrate on the new ideas in the professional journal you're reading.

Along with your scheduled investment in reading, you should build a relationship with your district curriculum coordinator. At the very least, the coordinator can help you look at what literacy-related issues are being considered by the district and the politics behind curriculum decisions being made. At the most, you'll have a confidante with whom you can brainstorm ideas concerning the visions and direction you want your school to take. You may want to take professional reading to the next level by engaging in a common reading with colleagues in leadership positions and getting together regularly in a social situation to discuss the nature and content of your shared reading.

When engaging in discussions with your colleagues about literacy, don't be afraid to admit ignorance. Christensen (1991) describes teaching and learning as "inseparable, parts of a single continuum—more Möbius strip than circle—of reciprocal giving and receiving" (p. 31). This metaphor can be extended to include the role of the school principal. What are principals if not teachers of an entire community?

To lead, a principal must model a willingness to shift from teacher to learner and to reflect openly on what each experience means. That being said, it's important to acknowledge what school leaders and their colleagues both in and around the classroom really talk about concerning literacy instruction. Do you have honest and regular conversations with the people you work with concerning where you would like your school to go in terms of literacy? Do you make the commitment to share with others your knowledge and questions about literacy and learning? Do you encourage others to do the same? When you set the tone for an environment that's open to learning about literacy, then your staff is more likely to ask questions that will lead to their own improvement and legitimately reflect on their own teaching.

Literacy in the community outside the school day is more than adult reading classes. Book talks are a wonderful way to start people thinking and talking about literature in groups and to share values about reading. Be mindful of the context in which book talks happen. Everyone tends to think of a book talk as a sterile, intellectual event. This doesn't have to be the case at your school. Make the effort to connect with your community by figuring out where they congregate and invite them to meet you there to discuss a book. Maybe your book talk happens in the middle of a bowling game, or maybe it happens over beer or coffee. Better yet, host a "Reading and Washing Saturday" at the local Laundromat, or ask to use the community room at a local apartment building. The point is to gently infuse reading into the daily lives of your community. Some of your community members will be thrilled at the idea of an intellectual exchange about a book over a glass of wine at a nearby restaurant, but this group usually won't represent all your community. Reading and discussions about reading should be nonthreatening events that people look forward to, regardless of their own literacy levels. Think about hosting book talks with your staff as well as members of your community. The books you select don't always have to be professional development books; also choose books that are fun to read and represent high literary qualities. The point here is that talking about reading should be fun as well as informative.

You also could host a reading exchange. Invite teachers, students, and families to save the magazines and books they read for a monthly swap at school. Set up tables with categories such as novels, gardening magazines, or picture books in the cafeteria or gym. When people enter the swap, they put their reading material in the proper categories and then are free to browse and take home items from other tables. This environmentally friendly practice promotes recycling, and it helps families build their libraries.

The ultimate integration of community literacy and school literacy are scenarios in which adults and children engage in activities based on a literacy theme. Events of this type are common in elementary school settings. Usually there's a school-wide drive in which, if so many books are read, a public figure (usually the principal) will promise to engage in some sort of mildly humiliating behavior such as kissing a pig or mud wrestling the resource officer. There are also national programs like Read Across America Day (also known as Dr. Seuss's birthday) annually observed on March 2. Some schools encourage students and faculty to come to school dressed as their favorite book character. Other schools host literacy-themed parades in conjunction with community centers, nursing homes, and shopping malls.

All of the above suggestions are meant to reinforce the idea that principals who are effective literacy leaders consistently step back from the immediate and daily demands of their school to think about their school and community in terms of global literacy values, about modeling their own values about literacy, and about making large systemic changes over time. Improving your school's literacy culture is an administrative marathon requiring the ability to see how one day's actions merge with other daily actions to affect a school over the course of months and years.

How do you lead literacy instruction?

Helping people to value and engage in literate behavior requires more than just telling folks that they should read. Teaching the value of literate behavior is something that must come across in both what you say and what you do. Think about what you do right now that demonstrates to your colleagues, students, and community that you value reading both personally and professionally. Brainstorm ways that your public library can truly become the heart of your community. An annual field trip to the library for every student to get a library card should be a given, and funding for such an activity can come from donations as well as community partnerships. Consider finding funds to reward students for outstanding behavior or other civic leadership by giving them subscriptions to age-appropriate magazines. Reward your teachers' outstanding efforts as well with gifts of journal subscriptions. All these actions will help to develop a culture that values literate behavior for all the constituencies you serve.

In terms of instructional leadership, you must face the fact that you're not omniscient and that you don't have to be. You'll be respected more if you model a consistent willingness to learn about instruction and to spread the word about what you've learned. It's also important to bear in mind the significance of embracing accountability both as a role model and as an evaluator of teaching. Furthermore, strong literacy programs reflect the very best practices in the teaching profession. By observing a literacy agenda for your school, you can truly reform your school community and ensure that your teachers are implementing the best approaches to teaching and learning.

Organization and consistency are particularly important in classroom observations and teacher evaluations; they make the difference between principals who are mediocre and those who truly are leaders. Invest the time to reflect on how you truly prioritize your day versus what you believe your values are about leading your school. Do you think that strong instruction is the most important thing at your school? If so, then you should be spending the majority of your time in the classroom observing your teachers and giving them feedback as well as support in the area of professional development.

Why is a literacy committee important, and who should be on it?

The final tool for creating a strong culture of literacy within a school is the development and maintenance of a literacy committee. This is a group that meets regularly, talks about the culture of literacy in the school community, and helps make decisions about what the school does to value and promote reading. We recommend that you use a shared leadership model for this committee. In this model, you form a group of no more than ten people representing teachers, parents, students, support staff, business leaders, and community service agencies (police, fire, veterans' organizations, community centers, retirement villages, and so on) that are part of your school neighborhood.

Empower this group to understand and value what you think is important concerning literacy, and let its members guide you in making decisions about literacy education in your school. This is the group with whom you need to build strong personal relationships that foster trust and a shared sense of commitment to improving the literacy culture of your school. These are the people who can help you to understand the Paradox of Educational Authority and how to fight effectively against it. Explore various ideas about literacy together with them. "Hot dot" what is valuable about literacy to these folks, and use that information to help set the direction your school is taking.

A viable literacy committee also ensures that you keep focused on issues concerning literacy throughout the year. By educating this committee, you help the community understand what is important to focus on. Perhaps one month you may teach the committee about struggling readers so that they better understand why your third-grade test scores are so low—or you might have a book talk about diversity to build empathy for teachers who work with students who come from print-free homes. Without a tool like the literacy committee, your community may not even understand what a print-free home is. This is also the group that will help you to convince others in the community that literacy education is the bedrock of an effective school and must be supported at all levels in the school and the community.

People who facilitate and lead a culture of literacy within their school communities are not all-knowing. Nor are they always the most well read. Rather, they are the professionals with a lifelong commitment to proselytizing and converting those around them to the intense, mind-opening experience that frequent visits to the literal or virtual pages of a book, magazine, or journal brings. Leading literacy instruction is indeed a calling.

Summary

Schools are complex organizations with multiple constituencies that demand a principal's time. One of the greatest challenges to school principals is to remember that instilling a vision requires first an understanding of what current values are within the various constituencies of a school community. Secondly, a principal must know his or her own values concerning literacy on both a personal and systemic level. Finally, effective principals who are literacy leaders examine the differences between literacy values within their constituencies and work to bring a harmonious understanding about what is currently valued in their school and what their school should and could value. We acknowledge that this juncture is only the beginning of a journey toward cultural literacy reform. However, it is a beginning that many principals overlook because they are unable or unwilling to regularly look at their school through an organizational lens in terms of the long-term and short-term investments and the impact they make on teaching and learning.

CHAPTER 2

How Do Children Learn to Read?

When Nancy and Gary Padak's children were young, they had a Friday evening ritual: popcorn, juice, and a movie. Until the night when this story took place, their youngest child, 3-year-old Matthew, ate dry cereal instead of popcorn because Nancy was concerned that popcorn might be dangerous for such a young child.

Matthew didn't care for this, and he nagged each week to be allowed to eat popcorn with his sister and brother. Finally, one night while they were in the kitchen microwaving the popcorn, Nancy gave in—but not before she gave him a "mom talk": "You're such a big boy. I know you'll take only one piece at a time and chew it very carefully," and so forth.

Matthew proudly toddled into the family room, popcorn bag in hand. His dad said, "What have you got there, Matthew?" Matthew replied, "Well, this is popcorn, and I can eat it. I can read it, too." Then, slowly dragging his chubby finger across the bag where the brand name was printed, he said, "Not for babies. Chew very carefully."

That's not what the bag said, of course, and prior to the 1970s when scholars began exploring what is now called *emergent literacy*, this would have been nothing more than a cute family story. However, think about what Matthew did in the context of learning to read. He showed that he knew quite a bit: Print carries a message; print goes from left to right; and reading is for communication. Those are important insights, developed naturally as Matthew participated as a member of a literate family. We now know that children like Matthew don't just learn to read at school; they have learned a great deal about written language before they enter school that provides a firm foundation for their literate futures.

Hence we include this chapter on how children learn to read, in which we provide a quick overview of several key concepts in the process. First, we present a brief description of some of the leading ideas or theories on how people read, what actually happens as they read. Second, we describe the learning-to-read process, both before school and in the primary years, along with brief explanations of certain within-the-child factors that are important to children's success in learning to read. Finally, we offer definitions and a few ideas for keeping current in the ever-expanding arena of "scientifically based reading research."

What, in a nutshell, is reading?

To understand the learning-to-read process, it's first important to think about what skilled or mature reading is; knowing where we want to go can help us understand the paths children take to get there. Many theories about how people read have come and gone over the years. At the risk of oversimplification, we describe three theories about how people read that are at the center of most current thinking. Each theory carries with it certain approaches to instruction that we'll address later in this chapter.

BOTTOM-UP THEORIES

In bottom-up theories, reading begins with the reader's perception of the smallest visual element of language–either the letter or, in some cases, only the features of letters. The reader then attends to progressively larger units of language, going from letters, to word parts, to words, to sentences, and so on, eventually arriving at the meaning of the text. This bottom-up, building-block reconstruction may begin with a reader sounding out a word, letter by letter, and then blending the sounds. Eventually, as readers become more proficient in recognizing letter combinations as words, they begin to identify whole words on quick examination of the array of letters in the word. This theory is often thought of as a part-to-whole approach to reading since readers use letter and sound cues to begin with small parts of reading and move to progressively larger parts until the end product, meaning, is developed.

TOP-DOWN THEORIES

Top-down theories can be thought of as the antithesis of bottom-up theories. In top-down theories, reading is based upon the reader's hypotheses about the meaning of the text as well as individual words. The hypotheses are tested using the visual cues in the text (letters, words, pictures, graphics) as well as using the meaning that develops as the text is read. The reader uses the ongoing meaning and knowledge of language to hypothesize about and identify upcoming words and meaning. Readers' overall familiarity with language, the language structures common in certain texts, different genres, and various life experiences help them make good hypotheses. For example, the words *Once upon a time* signal certain expectations or hypotheses about the text that is to follow. According to top-down theories of reading, these expectations or hypotheses about the meaning of the text drive reading, not the visual features of the print. Reading, then, is viewed as a whole-to-part process in which considerations of the whole text and whole meaning is followed by examinations of the parts.

INTERACTIVE PROCESSING

Do either of the preceding two theories appeal to your notion about how people actually read? Certain aspects of both appeal to us. We know that when we read we really do examine the words, and when we come to an unfamiliar word, we often try to sound it out or find familiar word parts within it. That's bottom-up processing. But we also know that reading is characterized by the process of making and testing predictions. Consider the following sentence fragment: *After the archery competition, the winner made another bow* . . . Are you able to read the fragment? No problem, huh? Well, what if the rest of the sentence looked like this: *to thank the audience for its applause.*

What did you do when you read the second half of the sentence? Did you take another look at the entire sentence? Did you change your pronunciation of *bow*? Did you even think about the two possible meanings and pronunciations for *bow* when you read the first part of the sentence? You probably hypothesized based on the meanings of the words that preceded it, but in this case, those words led you the wrong way. We most often notice predictions when they don't work out.

Some aspects about both theories of reading make sense so it makes sense to synthesize the two positions: Reading is an interactive process in which both bottom-up and top-down processing occur simultaneously.

Our cognitive systems are so well developed that we take on more than one operation at the same time; if one system breaks down, the other backs it up. You might think of this as "dual-action" reading.

There is more to this theoretical story than simple dual action. Keith Stanovich (1984) has argued that when it comes to identifying words, the bottom-up approach is much faster and more efficient than the top-down approach. According to Stanovich, effective word recognition is characterized by fast and efficient visual inspection; we identify words by matching them against our memory of the visual features of the words. When this process fails, we fall back on the less efficient top-down processing for word recognition. Thus, Stanovich's model is an interactive-compensatory model of reading. The process is interactive, but at the word level, the top-down processes compensate only when the bottom-up processes fail. So the best readers are those who are skilled in both strategies, bottom-up and top-down, for identifying words.

This doesn't mean that top-down processing is doomed to playing a secondary role in reading theory. Bottom-up processing applies only to the recognition of letters and words in print. Top-down processing has primacy, according to Stanovich, in nearly everything beyond word recognition. Comprehending the whole text, thinking about connections among individual chapters and paragraphs, monitoring understanding, predicting upcoming text, integrating new information with what we already know are all top-down processes. In these areas, which many argue are central to the reading process, readers combine their knowledge of the text, background experiences and prior knowledge, and knowledge of language to make and confirm predictions about text meaning, to monitor comprehension, to engage in meaningful text discussions with others, and to respond to the text in personally meaningful ways.

Thus, the most compelling theory of reading for us is one in which reading is a search for meaning. This search is guided by top-down, reader-initiated actions, but reading also involves the recognition of abstract printed symbols. Although this recognition can be accomplished by either top-down or bottom-up processing, bottom-up processing may be more

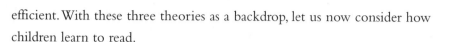

efficient. With these three theories as a backdrop, let us now consider how children learn to read.

How do children learn to read?

Many young children learn a great deal about reading in their preschool years, as Matthew's story at the beginning of the chapter illustrates. They begin to think about written language as a system, and they hypothesize about how it works. These understandings develop very early. Arthur Applebee (1978) found that by age two, children's responses to the directions *draw a picture* and *write a story* differ, with the latter looking somewhat like print, at least in layout.

Children also develop concepts about units of written language. They learn that print carries meaning and that we use certain rules or conventions of print to represent meaning. Eventually, they learn about the relationships among oral speech sounds and written letters. Children develop concepts about the reading process as well. Elizabeth Sulzby (1985) studied young children's "pretend reading" and discovered age-related stages, from looking at illustrations to looking at words and from "reading" that sounds like oral language to "reading" that sounds like written language.

This learning happens best in supportive and authentic environments. Children's learning is gradual and informal; the overall process involves hypothesis generation and testing. As they do with oral language, children try and then adjust their efforts, gradually moving closer to conventional representations. Like learning to talk, learning to read is a gradual, developmental process in which first attempts are approximations of skilled, mature behavior.

LEARNING TO READ IN SCHOOL

Although a great deal of the rest of this book is devoted to this topic, we do want to mention a few key ideas here, some notions that can provide a framework for your thinking about the process of supporting children's growing reading ability.

First, children build upon their notions about print and reading through authentic, engaged interactions with text and with others, including both the teacher and their peers. "Progress in becoming literate depends largely on the amount of time that students spend engaged in literate activity" (Rasinski & Padak, 2004, p. 4). Both time on task and the trickier issues of how much time on what kind of task, are related to this important concept.

The *Report of the National Reading Panel* (2000) has recommended the kind of tasks to focus on. Congress created the National Reading Panel (NRP) and charged it with reviewing instructional research in reading in preparation for the reauthorization of the Elementary and Secondary Education Act (now called *No Child Left Behind*). The National Reading Panel concluded that learning to read involves developing competence in four essential areas. These areas are defined below. (The quotes come from the Panel's Web site: http://nationalreadingpanel.org).

1. **Phonemic Awareness:** "Phonemes are the smallest units making up spoken language. English consists of about 41 phonemes. Phonemes combine to form syllables and words. A few words have only one phoneme, such as <u>a</u> (a) or <u>oh</u> (o). Most words consist of a blend of phonemes, such as <u>go</u> (g-o) with two phonemes, <u>check</u> (ch-e-ck) with three phonemes, or <u>stop</u> (s-t-o-p) with four phonemes. Phonemic awareness refers to the ability to focus on and manipulate these phonemes in spoken words."

2. **Phonics:** "Phonics instruction is a way of teaching reading that stresses learning how letters correspond to sounds and how to use this knowledge in reading and spelling. Phonics instruction can be provided systematically. Systematic phonics instruction occurs when children receive explicit, systematic instruction in a

set of pre-specified associations between letters and sounds."

3. **Fluency:** "Reading fluency is one of several critical factors necessary for reading comprehension, but is often neglected in the classroom. If children read out loud with speed, accuracy, and proper expression, they are more likely to comprehend and remember the material than if they read with difficulty and in an inefficient way."

4. **Vocabulary and Comprehension:** "Reading comprehension is very important to the development of children's reading skills and therefore to their ability to obtain an education. In carrying out its study of reading comprehension, the NRP noted three main themes in the research on the development of reading comprehension skills. First, reading comprehension is a complex cognitive process that cannot be understood without a clear description of the role that vocabulary development and vocabulary instruction play in the understanding of what has been read. Second, comprehension is an active process that requires an intentional and thoughtful interaction between the reader and the text (text comprehension instruction). Third, the preparation of teachers to better equip students to develop and apply reading comprehension strategies to enhance understanding is intimately linked to students' achievement in this area."

So the learning-to-read-in-school process should be characterized by authenticity, engagement, and a focus on essentials. In classrooms based on these major concepts, "teachers create conditions and develop activities that inspire students to read.... When students read willingly and teachers provide the necessary instruction, assistance, modeling, support, and encour-

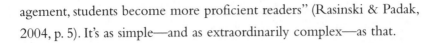

agement, students become more proficient readers" (Rasinski & Padak, 2004, p. 5). It's as simple—and as extraordinarily complex—as that.

How can we help children who struggle with learning to read?

Some children have always found (and probably will always find) learning to read difficult. Despite advances in our knowledge about effective reading instruction, we really don't know why. For some children, lack of preschool language and literacy experiences may be the "culprit." Other children may not be developmentally ready for the instruction that's offered to them.

Although we don't know why some children struggle to learn to read, we do know something about what sort of instruction can help them overcome their difficulties. We know, for example, that pull-out, skill-and-drill support isn't supportive at all (Allington, 1987, 2000; Allington & Walmsley, 1995). Children placed in these pull-out programs rarely improve sufficiently to overcome their early difficulties in reading. As an alterative, we recommend programs for struggling readers that are based on the following critical principles (Rasinski & Padak, 2004):

* Use authentic texts and other reading material.

* Focus on essential components of reading.

* Maximize reading of connected text.

* Provide for high levels of engagement.

* Focus on students' motivation and interest in reading.

* Make connections; help students see the role that reading can play in their out-of-school lives.

* Provide support when needed.

* Focus on success.

* Involve parents.

* Know students' abilities; track their progress.

Most children begin learning to read well before they enter school. School experiences based on authenticity, engagement, and a focus on the essential elements of reading help them grow and develop as proficient readers. Not all children are this fortunate, however, so helping struggling readers achieve success in reading must be among the most important goals of a school reading program. All these issues are threaded throughout the chapters of this book.

What key factors affect children's ability to learn to read?

This section contains a brief look at factors within children or their lives that are often associated with their success or lack of success in learning to read. Understanding these factors will help you help teachers develop and implement plans to ensure children's success.

FAMILY FACTORS

Our notion of family factors is broad: We mean the home and neighborhood environment, the family structure, relationships among family members, and even the literacy history of the family itself. Most important, though, are literate home environments and language interactions with children. Research tells us that the family plays an absolutely crucial role in children's development as learners (Padak & Rasinski, 2003), both before they enter school and during their school years. (Chapter 8 addresses family involvement in children's school learning. In this chapter, we focus on the preschool years.)

Until the late 1960s, reading methods texts typically advised teachers to keep parents away from reading-related issues. Reading was thought to be too complex; even well-meaning parents would likely hinder, not help, children's reading progress. Dolores Durkin (1966) changed all that. In a seminal study, she looked at children who learned to read before beginning school. She was fascinated by these precocious children and wanted to find out what led them to reading success at such an early age. Were they exceptionally brighter than their peers? Did parents provide instruction or use specialized teaching materials?

Durkin found none of the above. Instead she found that children who were early readers came from families that valued reading. In fact, reading was so important that at least one parent described himself or herself as an avid reader. The children were exposed to books and reading at an early age. Parents read to them daily, and they had access at home to lots and lots of reading material and writing material. Family members encouraged children to look at books and write their own. In short, parents created a home atmosphere where reading was valued. This created a desire in the child to participate in the family's literate lives, and the parents encouraged that participation by reading to the child. Parents didn't try to teach their child to read. It just happened. Children's early reading advantages followed them to school, where they continued to do well in reading.

Family language interactions are important as well. Parent-child talk promotes children's language development, helps children learn concepts, and creates a solid linguistic foundation for reading. Here, unfortunately, at least some of the news is grim. Researchers Betty Hart and Todd Risley (1995, 2003) wanted to learn more about the early language interactions in families of varying socioeconomic status (SES). They worked with 42 families (13 upper SES, 10 middle SES, 13 lower SES, 6 on welfare) for an hour per month over two-and-a-half years. During this time, they observed and tape-recorded parents talking with their young children. (Children were 7 to 9 months old at the beginning of the study and 36 months old at the end.) Hart and Risley transcribed and analyzed the tapes to learn more about family conversations and children's opportunities to learn through language.

"The acorn doesn't fall very far from the tree" describes one major finding. Hart and Risley found that the children grew "more like their parents in …vocabulary resources, and in language and interaction styles.… 86%-98% of the words in each child's vocabulary consisted of words also recorded in their parents' vocabularies" (2003, p. 7).

Another of their findings relates to the sheer number of words involved in parent–child talk. The chart below summarizes these findings. This stunning difference in children's access to language is perhaps the major finding of this important study.

WORDS PER TIME FACTOR	Children From Welfare Families	Children From Working-Class Families	Children From Professional Families
Per hour	616	1,251	2,153
Per week	62,000	125,000	215,000
Per year	3.2 million	6.5 million	11.2 million
In 4 years	13 million	26 million	45 million

Twenty-nine children from this original group of 42 were tested as third graders to explore the long-term results of their early language interactions. In 2003, Hart and Risley found that the children's rate of vocabulary growth and vocabulary use at age three was strongly associated with their third-grade standardized test scores in receptive vocabulary, listening, speaking, semantics, syntax, and reading comprehension.

Perhaps these brief summaries of only two important studies in this area can help you see why we referred to family factors as "absolutely crucial." For good or for ill, preschool family influences are strong. What's more, early interactions around reading have a profound affect on children's later reading achievement.

COGNITIVE FACTORS

At the turn of the 20th century, Edward Thorndike, an early educational psychologist, described reading as thinking. He believed that reading involves using one's cognitive processes to solve the problem of making sense of those written squiggles on the page. Clearly, reading is influenced by our ability to think, to understand our world. It may be helpful to understand, then, how cognition develops in young children. The people to go to for this information are Jean Piaget and Lev Vygotsky.

Piaget, perhaps the most important developmental psychologist of the past century, used observations of his own children to create a stage theory of cognitive development. He found that children's thought processes tended to move from a focus on self (sensori-motor stage, birth to age 2), to a more social self (preoperational stage, 2 to 7 years), to consideration of things concrete or physically at hand (concrete operational stage, 7 to 11 years), and finally, to the ability to consider mentally abstract (nonconcrete) ideas (formal operational stage, age 11 through adulthood). Piaget's theory posits that thought is initially focused on things in, on, or nearby the child and gradually begins to move outward to the point where the child can deal with ideas and notions that don't exist in the real world.

Helping a child learn to read and to deal with written language, then, means dealing with what is close to the child at first and gradually moving to more distant and abstract considerations. How can this be done? Piaget found that children learned about their world by acting on objects. With young children this means touching, but over time children's acting on things becomes less physical and more abstract. At any age, the ability to learn by acting on, by playing around with, or by experimenting remains an important way of learning, including learning to read.

Another of Piaget's important contributions to understanding cognitive development relates to how children think about objects. Early in life, their understanding of objects is holistic. Children see the entirety of objects rather than how the various parts might be put together. During the pre-operational stage (ages 2 to 7), children begin to understand part-to-whole relationships, to see how the forest and the trees are related. This ability is of considerable importance in reading. Some aspects of reading require the ability to deal with parts (words as parts of sentences, letters and syllables as parts of words) and to synthesize or to put those parts together into a meaningful whole. According to Piaget's theories, children will find this kind of thinking very challenging until they reach the concrete operational stage (ages 7 to 11).

The Russian psychologist Lev Vygotsky, a contemporary of Piaget's, has added to our understanding of cognitive development. According to Vygotsky (1962), cognitive and language development have a social dimension. Children's ability to think and talk develops through interactions with others. Collaborative experience, whether with other children or with an adult, is essential to children's cognitive development, including their reading development.

Vygotsky's notion of the *zone of proximal development* (ZPD) is also important for understanding cognitive development. The ZPD describes learning that is neither too easy nor overly frustrating. Children can learn moderately challenging ideas or skills with the assistance of another (e.g., teacher, parent, peer). The things that children can do with help from others, they can soon do on their own. According to Vygotsky, learning is most effective within this zone of proximal development. (By the way, another term we use in literacy instruction also refers to the same concept—the *instructional level*. The instructional level refers to learning tasks or texts that students are unable to complete independently but can complete successfully with assistance.)

It should be clear that the ability to think and skill at thinking contribute to our ability to read and to learn to read. Moreover, many of our understandings about how we think and how our cognitive skills develop have implications for how reading is taught. Both Piaget's theories about how children's thinking develops and Vygotsky's notions of the social aspects of learning and the zone of proximal development have direct implications for instruction.

LINGUISTIC FACTORS

Linguistic factors certainly affect the ability to learn to read. Think of two immigrants to this country, one who speaks no English and the other who does. Who has the more daunting task ahead? Even native English speakers' linguistic differences can affect reading development. Preschool interactions help children learn concepts and sentence structures; this is one reason why the Durkin and Hart and Risley studies, described earlier, are so important. Likewise, children whose oral language patterns differ from the mainstream school dialect may be unfamiliar with the words, sentence structures, and sounds of the school dialect.

Children need to control several aspects of language. Perhaps the most obvious is *phonology*, or the sounds of language. Children need some degree of control over the articulation of linguistic sounds. Of course, as children develop, the loss of teeth and the growth of their mouth cavities alter the quality of speech sounds they produce. We aren't too concerned about these; however, we should be concerned if children are unable to produce or to detect certain sounds in language. Since reading is, to some degree, dependent upon the readers' associating letters and letter combinations with sounds, learners' control over the sounds of language is important.

A second important aspect of language is *semantics*. Semantics refers to meaning extracted from language, whether of an individual word or a sentence, paragraph, or story. It can also refer to the denotative (literal) or connotative (figurative) meaning of an utterance. Your superintendent might say, "Nice job," for example, in two different ways depending on whether you had done well or not. Learners' ability to take meaning from language is critical to their development as readers, since the goal of reading is to make sense of the text. The semantic system plays other roles in reading as well. Often, by focusing on the meaning of a sentence, a reader can figure out an unknown word.

Consider the following: *For lunch today, I had a ham and TUYOIUIO sandwich.* Your sense of the meaning of the sentence, your semantic sense, probably helped you figure out the hidden word, or at least limit the possibilities. Although *cheese* was the word we had in mind, your semantic sense may also have led to *turkey, pickles,* or *mustard* (but not *tower, part,* or *must*) as possibilities. Thus, thinking about the sense of written text can help the language user at a number of levels and in a number of tasks.

Another aspect of language, *syntax,* is related to semantics. Syntax refers to word order. For example, noun phrases are ordinarily followed by verb phrases in English, adjectives or noun markers precede nouns, and so on. Syntax also helps us make sense of what we read. When we read *Tom hit Tim,* for example, syntactical knowledge allows us to know who got hit and who did the hitting. Like semantics, syntax can help with the identification of unknown words. Take for example the following sentence: *I am so hungry that I could eat a DRKSJ.*

Semantics helps us figure out that the hidden word refers to eating, but syntax provides important information too. Knowing that the hidden word is preceded by a noun marker (*a*) and that no words follow it tells us that syntactically the word is a noun.

Children's control over their language affects their ability to read. As they become readers, they need to learn how written language works. To mature as readers, they need opportunities to explore the complexities of written language. Fortunately, they have a wealth of linguistic information related to oral language to draw upon.

BACKGROUND KNOWLEDGE FACTORS

We've already discussed some aspects of background knowledge, e.g., cognitive and linguistic factors, and certainly, children's background knowledge is influenced by family interactions. Nevertheless, conceptual background knowledge is important enough for its own discussion. Research in the 1970s and 1980s has demonstrated quite clearly that the reader's background knowledge has a strong effect on reading. A rich background supports reading, and a limited background makes reading very difficult. Imagine reading a complex research article in an area outside your expertise, for example. You would have difficulty understanding the concepts and the connections between them. The implication is clear. In order to profit from reading, readers need to know something about what they are reading. Before children go to school, they gain this sort of background knowledge from their families by hearing stories, going on vacation or trips to the supermarket and zoo, and so on. However, the need for background knowledge does not cease upon school entrance; in fact, it's at least partially our responsibility to see that children have an ever-increasing store of background knowledge and conceptual knowledge.

AFFECTIVE FACTORS

Another cluster of very important factors that shape the learner's potential to successfully acquire literacy are affective. These include the learner's attitudes and motivation to learn to read; interests; beliefs about reading and learning to read; and emotional dispositions about reading, learning, and schooling. With regard to attitudes toward reading, McKenna and Kear (1989) found that elementary students' attitudes toward reading decline with every succeeding year. Something happens, and we suspect it happens in school, that leads students to becoming aliterate persons, people who can read but choose not to. Reversing this trend is one of the most important goals of an effective school reading program.

The affective dimension also includes how children think about themselves as readers, how they feel about reading rather than what they know about reading. Do they see themselves as good readers making progress, or do they believe they are poor readers? Psychologists who study motivation for achievement point to expectations for success and seeing value in the learning as critical. These affect persistence, which in turn affects learning (Wigfield & Asher, 1984). Certainly, motivation is related to both success and learning to find value in the activity, in this case reading. In fact, a series of studies conducted through the National Reading Research Center in the late 1990s established a synergy between motivation and ability—the two are mutually reinforcing phenomena (Baker, Afflerbach, & Reinking, 1996; Gambrell, 1996).

PHYSICAL AND SENSORY FACTORS

Reading is a physical and sensory activity; it involves the visual perception of written symbols and the auditory sense as written symbols are translated into speech. Beyond this, however, are preconditions for efficient learning such as being rested and free from hunger and having other basic physical needs met. Children also need to be able to pay attention to the teacher for reasonable periods of time. Easily distracted children may have difficulty focusing on the lessons and the information being presented to them.

Reading is a complex process, so it should come as no surprise that so many factors influence it. The effective teaching of reading depends upon a strong understanding of children, how they read, and the variety of factors influencing their development as readers. Research and well-developed research reviews can help develop this understanding.

What is scientifically based reading research?

With the publication of the *Report of the National Reading Panel* (NRP, 2000) and then the enactment of the *No Child Left Behind Act* (2001), some new jargon entered our field: scientifically based reading research. We are now told that instruction must be based on scientific research, which certainly makes sense, but what exactly is scientifically based reading research? This question has caused a great deal of controversy in the literacy field. In this brief section, we provide two definitions for you, one from the NRP and one from another highly regarded group, the National Research Council.

The NRP "first reviewed public databases and found about 100,000 research studies on reading that had been published since 1966. Because it was not possible for the Panel to critically review all this research, panel members decided to set criteria for which studies to include in their review." (See the NRP Web site: http://www.nationalreadingpanel.org.) The next step in their process was to identify topics of importance. Here the NRP was guided by the work of the National Research Council, specifically the summary report, *Preventing Reading Difficulties in Young Children* (Snow, Burns, & Griffin, 1998). "Once it selected the topics for review, the Panel also decided how to choose which studies to include in its analysis. To ensure the quality of the work, the Panel agreed to base its conclusions only on studies that had appeared in English in a refereed journal. The Panel limited its review to studies that focused directly on children's reading development from preschool through grade 12. The Panel also concentrated only on studies that were experimental or quasi-experimental in design. These studies had to include a sample size that was considered large enough to be useful, and the instructional procedures used in the studies had to be well defined." (See the NRP Web site: (http://www.nationalreadingpanel.org.)

What is scientifically based research? The National Reading Panel defined it very narrowly, much more narrowly than most literacy scholars would. No correlational or descriptive research was included, for example, so Durkin, Hart and Risley, and even Piaget were excluded. Most literacy scholars subscribe instead to a definition like the following, which comes from the National Research Council (2001, upon which the NRP based its work, if not its definition of scientifically based reading research):

"The design of a study (e.g., randomized experiment, ethnographic case study) does not make the study scientific. A wide variety of legitimate scientific designs are available for education research. They range from randomized experiments... to in-depth case studies... to neurocognitive investigations.... To be scientific, the design must allow direct, empirical investigation of an important question, account for the context in which the study is carried out, align with a conceptual framework, reflect careful and thorough reasoning, and disclose results to encourage debate in the scientific community." (p. 4)

We have two strong recommendations related to this issue. The first is that you adopt this second, broader definition of scientifically based reading research. It's widely accepted in the literacy research community. In fact, it's also the definition we adopted in deciding which research to share with you in this book. Our second recommendation relates to the decisions you make to guide your school reading program. We feel very strongly that such decisions must be based on research, if it's available. To do otherwise, we believe, is professionally irresponsible.

How can you keep up with current literacy research?

This is a daunting but critical task, and we have no simple suggestions for accomplishing it. However, we can offer the following advice:

* Find a trusted literacy expert in your school, district, or community (e.g., a professor). Ask him/her to share important research with you.

* Start or join a network of colleagues to review pertinent periodicals for peer-reviewed research that has instructional implications. Each person could select one journal to review. Together, your network can stay apprised of critical new research findings. Journals within the field of literacy education that may be particularly useful include *The Reading Teacher* and *Reading Research Quarterly* (published by the International Reading Association [IRA], www.reading. org), *Language Arts* (published by the National Council of Teachers of English [NCTE], www.ncte.org), the *Journal of Literacy Research* (published by the National Reading Conference [NRC], www.nrconline.org), and *Reading Research and Instruction* (published by the College Reading Association, www.collegereadingasso- ciation.org). More general journals, such as *Educational Leadership* (published by the Association for Supervision and Curriculum Development, www.ascd.org), *Phi Delta Kappan* (www.pdkintl.org), and *Elementary School Journal* (www.journals.uchicago.edu/ESJ/home.html), occasionally publish important articles in reading as

well. Obviously, keeping up with all these journals yourself would be unrealistic, but if you work with colleagues and adopt a "divide and conquer" mentality, you can do it.

* Look at Web sites for professional organizations occasionally. (See the Web sites given above.) IRA and NCTE publish research-based position statements, written and approved by their boards of directors. NRC sponsors a series of "White Papers" that are syntheses for general educational audiences written by prominent scholars.

* Attend a national literacy conference every few years. The IRA annual meeting, for example, features literally hundreds of sessions, most related to the elementary level. If you travel to the conference with a small team of teachers, the "divide and conquer" approach can enable you collectively to gather a great deal of research-based information in a relatively small amount of time.

Obviously this charge to keep current, while important, will take some of your time. We believe that this is an essential part of your role as a literacy leader within your school, however, and we urge you to develop a plan for staying abreast of important research findings related to how children learn to read and how schools and teachers can best support them.

Summary

Reading is complex, and so is learning to read. Fortunately, scholars have unraveled some of this complexity for us, and we've attempted in this chapter to share the essentials with you. We hope you'll remember to value what children bring with them to school, as well as the within-the-child factors that can influence their success as readers. We also hope you'll remember that reading is a meaning-making process, that all the instruction we offer children must be aimed at helping them learn to discover what authors are communicating to them. Finally, we urge you to insist upon research-based practices and programs in literacy. To do otherwise is, we think, professionally irresponsible.

CHAPTER 3

What Does an Effective Literacy Classroom Look Like?

During Nancy's second year of teaching, she had a group of recalcitrant readers. She knew that reading practice would lead to reading growth and that negative attitudes about reading might hamper the students' achievement, so she worked particularly hard during the first weeks of school to help combat these problems. She selected enticing read-alouds and often concluded reading for the day at an exciting point. Nancy found out about the students' interests and sought out reading material—books and magazines in those days—that she hoped they would find fascinating. She began a sustained silent reading (SSR) practice. She and her students initially read silently for only a few minutes each day; this time was gradually lengthened as the students could read for longer periods of time. At the end of the first month of school, Nancy was proud that her students could sustain their reading for 15 minutes each day and that many seemed displeased when SSR concluded.

As a nontenured teacher, Nancy was evaluated several times throughout the year. Her first evaluation was in mid-October, and she was pleased to see the principal, Mr. Pillon, arrive one day during SSR. "He knows these kids," she thought. "He'll be stunned to see them reading!" But Mr. Pillon surprised her. He walked in, looked around, and said in a booming voice, "I'll come back when there's something important going on." The principal did come back, and in their post-evaluation conference, Nancy had the chance to explain that developing reading habits was important. After their conversation, Mr. Pillon felt bad. "I wish I had known," he said.

Mr. Pillon is not alone. Over ten years ago, Jacobson, Reutzel, & Hollingsworth (1992) surveyed more than 1,000 elementary principals to determine their understanding of current issues in the field and the sources of information they use to stay current. One conclusion from that study seems as relevant today as it was then: "principals ... need readily accessible and practical information to significantly impact implementation of the current innovations in reading education" (p. 370).

We believe that "readily accessible and practical information" starts with instructional issues. Furthermore, we believe that the answer to what an effective literacy classroom looks like is made up of two parts. The first part is literal—we describe what you might see and hear in effective classrooms. The second part—perhaps the more important part—can't be readily seen. Like Mr. Pillon, you'll learn about these aspects of instruction through conversations with teachers.

We begin with ideas that apply to all classrooms and then describe some grade-related issues. We conclude with brief discussions of two other critical aspects of instruction: classroom and school libraries and technology.

What are the grounding literacy threads that should be in every classroom?

The five essential threads described below should be evident in every teacher's classroom. These essentials may be manifested in different ways in different rooms, but every class should address them, as they provide a depth of learning for all classrooms based on literacy-centered curriculum.

1. Reading instruction should be authentic and engaging.

You should see and feel excitement about reading in every teacher's classroom. Children should be actively involved as successful readers. The teacher's enthusiasm for reading should be readily apparent, as should his or her expectation that all children will be successful. You should feel that you're entering a community of learners when you walk through the classroom door. These characteristics should be apparent in instruction for all students—those who read well above grade level and those who struggle.

2. Reading instruction should focus on both skill and will.

With regard to skills, expect to find the focus on phonemic awareness and phonics in K–1 classrooms and on fluency, vocabulary, and comprehension in all classrooms. In addition, from grade 3 (or so) onward, teachers should be helping students to learn independently. Skills instruction should focus on application; that is, children should be led to consider how a new skill can be used to help them read better. In a way, then, "skills instruction" is a bit of a misnomer; "strategy instruction" may be the better label (National Reading Panel [NRP], 2000).

"Will" is equally important in reading instruction. Correlational studies have provided strong evidence that children who are better readers read more than children who struggle as readers (Postlethwaite & Ross, 1992). Surely positive attitudes about reading contribute to wanting to read—and those who want to read will find time to do so. Beyond students' achievement in school, most of us would acknowledge that our long-term goals include helping children become avid readers for life. Students' positive attitudes about reading (and themselves as readers) are important here too, so you should see evidence of focus on both skill and will in each classroom. Instruction should provide scaffolding for children's growing independence as readers. Teachers should be actively modeling and demonstrating useful strategies (Allington, 2002). Discussions about text should feel more like conversations than oral tests. Moreover, a "can-do" attitude should prevail, and children's enthusiasm for reading should be apparent.

3. Students should have ample time each day to grow as readers.

Most reading scholars identify time as an essential element of instruction. Dick Allington (2002), for example, notes that children in the classrooms of the outstanding teachers he observed often spent up to 50 percent of their school day reading and writing. Not all of this occurred during reading time, of course—children read and wrote in science, social studies, and even math. Nonetheless, children should be reading and writing for at least a couple of hours during each school day (Cunningham, Hall, & Defee, 1998; Shanahan, 2000).

How reading time is spent also deserves mention, and here the notion of balance is useful. You should expect to find some focus on word study (phonics for younger children; spelling and vocabulary instruction for all children), fluency, and comprehension. Students should have time to read independently and to interact with classmates, but they should also be involved in instruction guided by the teacher (Cunningham et al., 1998; Shanahan, 2000).

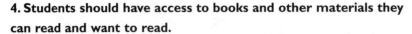

4. Students should have access to books and other materials they can read and want to read.

In our area of the country, we are encountering more and more teachers and students who are increasingly frustrated by school or district mandates that only grade-level materials be used for reading instruction. Such mandates are effective only for a fraction of students in any classroom, those who can read the materials successfully with the teacher's help. Some students in most rooms read above the grade-level text. They don't need the teacher's help and have little to learn about reading strategies and skills since they don't need to solve problems as they read. In contrast, some students in most rooms read below grade level, so attempting to work with a grade-level text only brings frustration and failure.

We suspect that these grade-level mandates are well meaning. It would be wonderful if all children could read on grade level. Although this goal is a worthy one, wishing doesn't make it so. We have known for more than 50 years that children can progress most rapidly as readers when they work instructionally with materials that are challenging but not frustrating (Betts, 1946). Operationally, this challenging-but-not-frustrating level, called the "instructional level" in reading circles, is characterized by good, but not excellent, word recognition (at least 90 percent); good, but not excellent, comprehension; and reasonable (good, but not excellent) fluency. In other words, when reading at their instructional levels, children encounter some problems and can use their teacher's help but are not so overwhelmed with difficulties that the reading experience is dreadful for them. A much better mandate, then, would be to require that instruction be based on assessment of students' instructional levels and that all children receive the teacher's assistance in reading texts that are challenging but not frustrating.

If we want to "grow readers," we also need to provide plenty of opportunities for students to read stories, poems, essays, Web pages, nonfiction of all kinds, and other authentic texts. These reading experiences can help them learn that reading is enjoyable and has meaning in their lives. Many of the materials available as part of commercial reading programs offer little enjoyment or satisfaction for students, nor is their applicability to real-life reading readily apparent. Although such materials may be used occasionally for instruction, students should also have time and support each day to read what they want to read.

5. Instruction should be planned to meet students' needs.

As might be evident from the above, it's important for instruction to meet students' needs. This can only be accomplished if assessment is part of each teacher's routine. Here we do not refer to formal tests, although they are a fact of life in most schools. Instead, we refer to the informal assessments that can help teachers see what children know and are able to do and where lack of knowledge, skills, or strategies might be hampering their progress as readers. Effective teachers provide support or scaffolding to make reading manageable and meaningful for students, to help individuals grow in reading competence. And since individuals' needs differ, this support can take many forms. This may mean reading to or with students before asking them to read the text on their own, ensuring that they have sufficient background knowledge to understand the text, checking that the text is sufficiently easy for them to read, or asking them to practice reading a passage at home with their parents before reading it at school. Readers should never struggle to the point of failure or frustration in any reading task or activity (Rasinski & Padak, 2004).

All children, even those reading above grade level, can advance as readers. Indeed, reading achievement continues well beyond elementary school into middle school, high school, and beyond, so you should expect to find evidence of instruction that meets all students' needs. Teachers should be able to talk to you about how they plan instruction, and you should find evidence of their use of informal assessments in their explanations.

What does an exemplary teacher's classroom look like?

How do all these essentials or "big ideas" come together? Several researchers have explored this very question by learning from exemplary teachers, those whose students consistently achieve much more than expectations. Compared to the classrooms of their less successful peers, these teachers' classrooms were characterized by the following:

* Excellent classroom management and a positive, cooperative tone

* Easy access to abundant materials for reading

* Coaching, scaffolding, and explicit skills instruction. Teachers' instruction focused on authentic application of skills and was challenging but not frustrating for students. Lots of higher-order questioning (e.g., inferences, integration, application) was evident.

* Academically busy atmospheres, with children spending lots of time engaged in real reading, real writing, and independent and cooperative learning

* Greater outreach to parents; more emphasis on bringing the "outside world" in to the classroom (Pressley, Allington, Wharton-McDonald, Block, & Morrow, 2001; Taylor, Pearson, Clark, & Walpole, 2000)

What are the key effective instructional practices?

With these big ideas as a backdrop, we next move to brief overviews of effective instructional practices in decoding, fluency, and comprehension. If you want more information about these critical areas (and we hope you do!), the citations within these brief explanations point to a great deal of additional research, information, and insights.

EFFECTIVE DECODING INSTRUCTION

Boy, is this a contentious area of reading instruction! It seems to us that questions about how, when, and for whom decoding should be taught are responsible for a great deal of controversy surrounding reading instruction, both now and in years past. In this section, we provide some basic definitions and guidelines for instruction. You can look to other resources (e.g., Bear, Invernizzi, Templeton, & Johnston, 2000; Rasinski & Padak, 2001) for added detail.

Almost all literacy scholars see the need to teach children to decode unknown words, and phonics, the process of associating written letters with sounds, is nearly always seen as important to decoding. The *how* and *when* of phonics instruction are a bit more controversial. In brief, scholars are divided about whether sounds should be taught in isolation, often called *synthetic phonics*, or with a focus on words and word families, often called *analytic phonics*. We have our own preferences, but we believe it's important for you to know that research is not yet clear about this aspect of the *how* question. One conclusion from the National Reading Panel (NRP), though, is that phonics instruction should be systematic and not haphazard.

With regard to the *when* of phonics instruction, debate now seems to center on when it should end (some time in the primary years; the NRP says early) rather than when it should begin. We suspect that this is due to a relative newcomer on the scene—phonemic or phonological awareness, the ability to recognize, segment, and blend the sounds of oral language. Recent research suggests that phonemic awareness is an important precondition for learning phonics (Adams, 1990; NRP, 2000), so kindergarten classes now feature attention to phonemic awareness. Some children come to school already phonemically aware, so they do not need this instruction. For those students who lack phonemic awareness, the NRP conclusions suggest that just a few minutes of instruction each day should suffice and that phonemic awareness activities seem to be more successful when they're linked to helping children learn letters of the alphabet. Again, some children come to school with this knowledge, so you should expect to find some differentiation of instruction in kindergarten classes.

Steven Stahl (1992) identified several research-based principles to guide phonics instruction. Instruction should do the following:

* Proceed from what children already know about language and reading

* Be clear, direct, brief, and focused

* Focus on reading words rather than learning rules

* Feature opportunities for children to manipulate and experiment with letters and sounds

You might expect to find these principles in practice in the first- and second-grade classrooms in your building. Some kindergartners, especially in the spring of the year, will also be ready for phonics instruction. Sifting through the controversy regarding decoding instruction can be a full-time job. Rather than concerning yourself with these arguments, we suggest that you talk with your teachers about their instruction. Learn about the *why* and *how* and pay attention to the extent to which teachers' decisions rest on research-based principles, both those mentioned above and others that they share with you.

EFFECTIVE FLUENCY INSTRUCTION

Fluency is the ability to read expressively and meaningfully, as well as accurately and with appropriate speed. Fluency is important because it enables comprehension. In fact, research into repeated readings, a common fluency instructional activity, indicates that it not only leads to improvement in the practiced text but also to improvements in decoding, reading rate, and comprehension of unfamiliar texts (Dowhower, 1994; Herman, 1985; Koskinen & Blum, 1984, 1986; Kuhn & Stahl, 2000; NRP, 2000). This reading practice transfers to new, unread text.

Unfortunately, studies have also found that significant numbers of students are not fluent readers. In 1995, Pinnell et. al. concluded that 45 percent of U.S. fourth graders read below minimally acceptable fluency levels. Only 13 percent of these fourth graders read at the highest fluency level. So from both perspectives—importance to reading growth and apparent student weaknesses in this area—fluency deserves instructional emphasis at every grade level.

You should expect teachers to spend ten to fifteen minutes each day on fluency instruction and practice. They should not concentrate solely on increasing the rate of reading. In fact, emphasizing speed at the expense of expressive and meaningful reading leads to fast readers who understand little of what they've read. You should see a focus on meaningful interpretation on the part of students, as well as teachers' efforts to weave fluency work into other areas of the school curriculum. These efforts may take several forms, such as the following:

* The teacher models fluent reading. You might expect teacher read-alouds to be great examples of expressive, fluent reading. Moreover, you might expect teachers to talk with children about how understanding can be enhanced through fluent reading.

* The teacher provides fluency support. Hearing fluent reading is not the same as being a fluent reader. Thus, assisted reading, another method associated with

fluency improvements (Kuhn & Stahl, 2000; NRP, 2000), should be another important component of the fluency program. Several methods for assisted reading show promise. One is a simple routine that begins with the teacher reading a short text to students. Then students follow along silently as the teacher reads the text aloud again. Group (choral) reading is next, after which students may read aloud to partners.

* The teacher encourages repeated readings. Practice makes perfect in reading in the same way it does in other areas such as playing a musical instrument. Repeated readings work best when students have an authentic reason—performance—for all that practice (Samuels, 1979). Children need to practice reading texts that lend themselves to performance like poetry, scripts, speeches, monologues, dialogues, and jokes or riddles. Storybooks may be good choices for fluency practice too, especially if students eventually read them to a younger audience. Of course, students will also need opportunities to perform for an audience.

* The teacher has a fluency routine. All these ideas will be most effective when they're bundled into a predictable routine. Several instructional routines for fluency have shown great promise for improving reading for all. Fluency Oriented Reading Instruction (Stahl & Heubach, 2005) focuses on passages from basal readers. The Fluency Development Lesson (Rasinski & Padak, 2005; Rasinski, Padak, Linek, & Sturtevant, 1994) uses poetry, monologues, dialogues, speeches, and other performance texts. Fast Start, described more completely in Chapter 8, promotes early reading fluency through parental involvement. Research has shown that each

of these routines is effective in promoting children's fluency growth and overall reading achievement.

EFFECTIVE COMPREHENSION INSTRUCTION

Comprehension, or the construction of meaning from text, has been defined as the process of "building bridges between the known and the new." This metaphor suggests that instruction should focus on both sides of this bridge, on what students already know about a topic and on what they can learn by reading. You might think of comprehension instruction as occurring before students read, as they are reading, and after they have read.

You should expect teachers to work to build background for (and interest in) a text before asking students to read and understand independently. Methods for building background knowledge include information sharing or class/group brainstorming. Several quick instructional activities, such as word sorts of various kinds (Rasinski & Padak, 2004), are useful for building interest as well as sharing information before reading. Many of these activities focus on two critical questions: *What do you think? Why do you think so?*

These questions also can provide comprehension support while students read and after they read. In fact, the NRP (2000) identified questioning as perhaps the most powerful strategy for improving readers' comprehension. These are not test-type questions, though; rather, students generate their own questions about the text or author before, during, and after reading the text.

In an effective classroom, you also might expect to see some emphasis on "nonlinguistic representation" (Marzano, Pickering, & Pollock, 2001), using imagery, sketches, graphics, and so on to support comprehension either during or after reading. Likewise, students may write either during or after reading, and this may serve as a note-taking function or as a means of reflection. As with before-reading activities, a nonlinguistic representation or a writing activity can take many forms.

After-reading activities typically focus on summarizing and synthesizing or reflecting. Working individually or in small groups, students focus on putting their insights into their own words, which helps them prioritize, recast, or learn. This after-reading activity should center frequently on making comparisons or connections, either between and among texts or from "text to self" or from "text to world" (Keene & Zimmermann, 1997).

In the early years, much comprehension instruction may surround teacher read-alouds. In older grades, children may interact with one another in literature circles, so the specifics of instruction may change from grade to grade. What should not change, though, is the major instructional focus on comprehension. After all, comprehension is the reason we read.

How does literacy instruction look across grade levels?

In this section, we summarize much of the preceding information by describing what you might expect to see in effective teachers' classrooms across the grades. We focus on the physical environment including classroom libraries, and the instructional routines that together might constitute a reading program. We then address two all-school issues: the school library/media center and the use of technology.

READING IN KINDERGARTEN

The physical environment in a kindergarten classroom should send positive messages about reading and learning. You might expect to find a place for whole-group instruction, centers for independent work, and little gathering areas for children to work together. You also might expect to find a library center consisting of baskets of books and places for children to read or look at them. On the walls, you might see alphabet letters, word walls of words that children know, charts using words to accomplish classroom business (e.g., attendance charts, library check-out areas), and lots of child-generated print. Overall, the classroom should be arranged to facilitate instruction, but more importantly, it should engage children's curiosity in reading and learning.

Of course, the library center should be a featured aspect of the classroom. Library centers with lots of inviting books, coupled with teachers' planned activities with the books, lead to kindergartners' interest in books (Morrow, 1982; Taylor, Blum, & Logsdon, 1986). In addition to providing opportunities for children to read or look at books independently, these planned activities might include frequent teacher read-alouds, perhaps coupled with comprehension activities. Some books should have predictable formats since repeated readings of predictable texts will foster children's ability to read them independently. Language experience activities, which feature children's dictation of texts that they then read and work with in other ways, might also be a frequent instructional routine.

Kindergarten teachers should help children learn reading skills and strategies, too, based on what they know about children's needs. A spirit of playfulness should be evident in this "skills" work. As noted above, this might include phonemic awareness activities, but you should also see evidence of instruction focused on helping children learn about how print works (words, letters, lines, and so on). Some of this instruction might be paired with fluency work so that children reread a particular text (for fluency) and then examine its parts (for word study). Finally, children should have frequent opportunities to write or draw or both, and they should be encouraged to create approximations for words as this practice leads to success in word recognition and, eventually, traditional spelling (Templeton & Morris, 1999).

READING IN PRIMARY GRADES

Some aspects of the kindergarten environment should still be apparent in primary classrooms: the print-rich, inviting nature of the room arrangement; a setup that encourages children's independence; walls and bulletin boards covered with child-generated materials; and spaces for cooperative work as well as whole-group instruction. And, as with kindergarten, the classroom library is important. Research has shown that classrooms of the primary teachers who "beat the odds" have clearly defined, well-stocked book areas and lots of child-produced print (Loughlin & Ivener, 1987; Pressley, Rankin, & Yokoi, 1996).

Teachers and children should spend at least two hours each day in reading-related activity. Among the instructional routines you might expect to find are the following:

* Teacher read-aloud

* Lots of time and encouragement for children to interact with books

* Focused efforts to develop children's fluency

* Whole-group and small-group comprehension discussions

* Instruction focused on developing decoding and comprehension skills and strategies

* Instruction and activities to foster children's vocabulary development

* Content-area literacy (e.g., science, social studies) instruction

* Opportunities for children to write

READING IN INTERMEDIATE GRADES

In the intermediate grades, the classroom setup should invite student independence in reading and writing. Reference books and computers with Internet connections should be readily available, and students should have reading/study areas for their independent inquiry. As with the classroom environment at other grade levels, research has shown the library center to be a critical aspect of intermediate grade classrooms. For example, library centers with lots of inviting books, coupled with teachers' planned activities, lead to vocabulary gains for low-SES students at grades 2, 4, and 6 (Snow,

Barnes, Chandler, Goodman, & Hemphill, 1991). Instructional routines will parallel those in the primary grades, although the skills and strategies that provide focus for instruction will be more complex or sophisticated, and the texts that students read will be more challenging.

What do all these classroom descriptions have in common? Instruction focuses on what children need. They have plentiful opportunities to read, both independently and with others. Students' responses to what they have read are valued. Teachers provide support, including direct instruction when needed, to assist each child's growth toward reading proficiency. And, of course, the classroom library is a critical aspect of the physical environment at all grade levels.

SCHOOL LIBRARIES/MEDIA CENTERS AND THE READING PROGRAM

School libraries/media centers have a critical role to play in developing children's literacy abilities. The school librarian/media specialist is an important resource for school-wide literacy improvement. This person should be an expert in children's/young adult literature and, therefore, helpful as teachers plan to engage children with books. Partnerships with classroom teachers and adequate library holdings appear to be the critical issues. One large study of the relationship between school library characteristics and students' reading achievement (Lance, Rodney, & Hamilton-Pennell, 2000), for example, identified the following factors that are significantly related to students' reading achievement: adequate staffing and staff credentials, school library expenditures, focus on information technology, and staff activities that link classroom and library curricula.

Library professionals also can serve as "diagnosticians" for classroom libraries. As we discussed before, rich and inviting classroom libraries are an essential element of effective teachers' classrooms. As Hoffman, Sailors, Duffy, and Beretvas (2004) put it, "There appears to be consensus within the field of reading as to the importance of classroom literacy environments in literacy development" (p. 304). School librarians/media specialists can help their classroom colleagues evaluate their classroom libraries and make plans for improvement. The table that follows is adapted from Hoffman et. al. (2004), who used it in a large-scale observation study and found, in all cases, that "outstanding" classroom libraries were associated with higher student achievement in reading. Classroom teachers and/or school librarians can use the table as a useful beginning to evaluate classroom library holdings.

ASPECT	INADEQUATE	BASIC	OUTSTANDING
Quantity	1–7 books/child	8–19 books/child	20+ books/child
Variety	10% or less nonnarrative	10%-20% nonnarrative	20%+ nonnarrative
	Less than 30% published in last 3 years	30%-50% published in last 3 years	50%+ published in last 3 years
	no multiple copies	few multiple copies	many multiple copies

For all these reasons, we recommend that you consider the school library/media center an important resource in your overall literacy education program. Moreover, library/media professionals should be regarded as key players in the development of your school literacy leadership team.

TECHNOLOGY AND THE READING PROGRAM

Take a minute to think about how the computer age has changed the ways we learn and communicate. Obviously, school reading programs must include emphasis on learning how to use technological resources. Two findings from the Lance et al. (2000) statewide study of library resources and student reading achievement underscore this point: "The most dramatic statistical difference between lower and higher achieving schools is in the area of information technology" (p. 19). Higher-achieving schools have more computers and are more likely to have them networked to each other and to the Internet. In addition, "higher and lower scoring elementary schools are distinguished by the amount of time school library staff spend in teaching students and teachers how to access and use print and electronic information resources" (p. 19).

Research focusing on instructional uses of computer technology is still in its infancy, but in 2000, the National Reading Panel was able to locate and evaluate approximately two dozen studies of the role of computers in classroom reading instruction. From this review, panel members were able to find general, positive support for classroom computer uses, particularly for word processing and reading hypertext. Until more research is available, however, we suggest that you not expect computers or computer programs to be the foundation of your school's reading program. Rather, as suggested throughout this chapter, teacher skill, a balanced curriculum, and easy access to fascinating texts appear to be the key ingredients to an effective reading program.

Summary ⵇⵌ

Learning to read is complex. Teaching reading is complex. Providing leadership for both groups—the learners and the teachers—is likewise complex. Yet your role in the school reading program is absolutely critical. Principals who demonstrate positive language arts leadership influence children's literacy learning in positive and significant ways. The possibilities are endless and exciting!

Chapter 3: What Does an Effective Literacy Classroom Look Like?

75

CHAPTER 4

How Do You Evaluate the Literacy Classroom?

When Autumn Tooms was an assistant principal at an elementary school in Arizona, she learned a lot about how principals evaluate literacy instruction—the hard way. During the summer of her second year in administration, the principal retired, and Autumn was part of the search committee to find a new leader for the school. The school she served was located in a community of trailer parks, strip clubs, crack houses, and a few small, middle-class homes. Teaching children how to read was a lower priority at this school than ensuring a safe learning environment. However, the district wanted to hire a principal who could really turn around the academic performance of the student body.

The committee charged with selecting the next principal consisted of the four parents who were involved in the school, a district office representative, and Autumn.

The hiring committee unanimously selected as their new principal a man who was currently serving as an assistant principal in a neighboring, ritzy school district that boasted some of the highest standardized test scores in the state. For the sake of this accounting, we will call this new principal Randy Firmi (a pseudonym).

Randy was charming and held himself with an air of authority. Several committee members commented that he really seemed to know a lot about instruction and curriculum. Randy's vocabulary was peppered with phrases like *You know the key is phonemic awareness . . .* or *In my old district, we really saw whole language as more than just loving books at a primary level.* Because Randy confidently wove into his discussions references to phonemes, diphthongs, and literacy researchers like Pinnell, Pressley, and Slavin, Autumn was a little intimidated. As a former chemistry teacher, she had no training in literacy, even though she was responsible for evaluating half the faculty.

Then one day in December, Autumn and Randy were reviewing the previous year's test scores. Randy commented that the staff just had a horrible approach to literacy. Autumn seized the moment and admitted to him that she really didn't understand that much about literacy instruction. Randy responded to the admission by holding up a basket filled with copies of *The Reading Teacher* and saying, "These can really help a lot."

Autumn quickly looked through a few copies of the journal and said, "Okay. I'll get a subscription, but what makes a good lesson? I don't think I know what I'm looking at." Randy curtly answered, "Well, you know it's complicated. It's very important that you see vocabulary words on the bulletin board in the classroom and that the children are focused on good literature. And then there's the importance of picking a quality book for discussions with them. In my old district, we really focused on the importance of phonemes and the whole language approach to words."

Autumn asked, "What's the difference between phonemic awareness and whole language? I don't understand."

Randy replied, "Well as I said, it's complicated ... but I look at it like going from part to whole and whole to part, and what's important is that the kids end up with an appreciation of quality literature."

Autumn felt like an idiot. She didn't understand a single word Randy had said, and she was too embarrassed to ask more questions. Furthermore, she felt that her boss was irritated with her questions about literacy, so she decided to excuse herself to supervise afternoon dismissal at the bus loading area.

Autumn was in the middle of helping the first graders get on a bus when Faye Reynolds, one of the most respected teachers on the staff, walked up. Faye was a terrific teacher with 20 years of experience, and Autumn valued her insights. Faye gently expressed her exasperation with Randy's lack of depth when it came to understanding reading instruction. To add to this frustration, Faye noted that the school district was gearing up for a new reading program adoption, and the teachers' sense of confidence in Randy's abilities as a curriculum leader were quickly waning.

Right then, Autumn learned the most important lesson about the evaluation of instruction: You can't fake it with teachers. Here was the unfortunate result of an administrator not being able cope with the ugly side of the Paradox of Educational Authority. Eventually, people figure out if you know what you're talking about or if you're pretending. The secret to true curriculum leadership is that you don't have to know everything. Being the instructional leader of a school is really about sliding along a continuum of learner, teacher, and motivator. You have to be able to admit your limitations concerning literacy instruction (or any other subject) and model a willingness to learn. Good principals support a commitment to learning along with clear, concrete expectations for staff in terms of the delivery of instruction. The purpose of this chapter is to discuss exactly how one sets those expectations and evaluates teaching.

What do you really know about literacy?

Before you can set expectations for your staff, you have to feel confidant about what you believe is important in literacy instruction. Learn from the mistake that Autumn's principal made and avoid jacking up your vocabulary with literacy jargon if you cannot clearly explain what you believe about literacy instruction. If you knew nothing about literacy before you picked up this book, really study the information in Chapters 2 and 3. We called this book an essential guide for a reason: Chapters 2 and 3 really are the nuts and bolts of what you should minimally know. As we've stated before, the more opportunities a child has to read, the more fluent he or she becomes, and the more likely he or she is to develop good literacy habits.

Additionally, you need to have some understanding of how your school district approaches literacy instruction. One of the wisest investments you can make is to build relationships with your fellow principals and your curriculum director. Have conversations with them about what the district, and they, value in terms of literacy instruction. Is there a reading program that was recently adopted? What do your colleagues think about it? What are its perks and its glitches? Don't discount the value of talking to your staff. Who on your staff really knows about reading? How do you know that they're experts? Are they routinely involved with district literacy issues? What are their perspectives on the literacy goals and programs prevalent in your district's culture?

Another way to decide what you think is important in terms of literacy instruction is to read about it with consistency. *The Reading Teacher,* sponsored by the International Reading Association, is the premier professional journal dedicated to the subject of literacy. Joining professional associations also can help broaden your perspective. Finally, don't be shy about contacting the university closest to you and asking their literacy professors a few questions. The point is that all these efforts will help you cement in your mind the things you'd like to see in your teachers' classrooms.

Help yourself form these global beliefs about literacy by writing them down. These beliefs will evolve into your expectations for staff. Take the time to sit by yourself, uninterrupted, and make a chart for every grade level in your school. On each chart, write the following categories:

* important activities that should happen each day

* classroom goals that the teacher should be focused on

* community goals that the teacher should be focused on

* help for struggling readers

Next, fill out these charts yourself. You can expect to see different items for each grade level in some categories and similar responses in others. For example, a classroom goal you might have is for all your teachers is to build and use a library in their classes. You also may decide that every teacher needs to make an effort to have students and their families read together at the school four times a year. This would fall under community goals for all grades. However, the parents of kindergartners might come to school for pajama reading at 7:00 in the evening and eighth graders' families might attend a poetry slam at school. A goal transcending two categories might be to have students in the upper grades work with students in the lower grades to practice their reading skills. Thus, struggling readers in lower grades have the opportunity to practice their skills, and students in the upper grades have the opportunity to meet a literacy goal based in the community.

Next, make a chart that lists what you want to see when you visit a classroom, such as the following:

* The objective of a lesson is written on the chalkboard so students and the teacher can remain focused on the purpose of the lesson.

* Vocabulary words for the week and/or day appear.

* Current student work is displayed, with evidence that student projects link literacy to other curriculum areas.

* Evidence that students are able to use their classroom environment independently, without having to ask the teacher to "get this" or "get that" every two minutes.

The final chart to make for yourself outlines the kinds of things that you absolutely *do not* want to see in a classroom visit. Here are few items to include on that list:

* A teacher who stays in one place and never moves during a lesson.

* A teacher reading to a group of students who are not engaged (e.g., they're sleeping or playing with each other).

* No student work is displayed or the work displayed is not current. (Six weeks is too much time to keep the same student work on display.)

* Student materials aren't organized.

* There's a lack of reading material for students who have finished an assignment.

Augment your charts by including what you've learned about what your district honors concerning literacy. For example, in Autumn's district, a value was placed on delivering instruction in both Spanish and English, so when she visited classrooms, she looked for displays and materials in both languages. Another example of a school-wide value in Autumn's school was a commitment voiced by the staff to explore the concept of democracy.

Thus, Autumn looked for evidence in every class that at some point in the day students were learning about various aspects of democracy.

When you've completed these charts on what you value in literacy, the next step is to cull this list to a manageable number (between three and four) of the most important items. Ultimately, you should end up with a chart like the following that reflects both your beliefs and what your school district values:

* Three daily activities that should be met by each grade

* Three classroom goals that each grade should be focused on

* Three community goals that each grade should be focused on

* Three goals for struggling readers that each grade should be focused on

* Three things you want to see in every classroom

* Three things you don't want to see in any classroom

The next step is to communicate these expectations to your staff. The perfect time to start the process of setting these expectations with them is at the August back-to-school faculty meeting, and the best way to present these expectations is clearly and in writing. Share your excitement about what your staff does in the classroom and offer your rationale for why you've selected these particular expectations. This process is a natural counterpart to the initial literacy value exercises outlined in Chapter 1 in that these reflections are more specific to instructional practices. The reflections in Chapter 1 are more specific to personal and cultural values about literate behavior.

How do you get teachers to meet expectations?

The first step in this process is to utilize lesson plans. If you don't already require your staff to give you lesson plans, consider the benefits of doing so. Lesson plans are a wonderful vehicle for teachers to communicate with the principal what they're doing and to think about their own teaching at a deeper level. Yes, it is a pain to get all teachers to turn them in. Yes, lesson plans are a pain to review. However, you need to consider lesson plans as a tool to help set and meet expectations with your staff. The reason that a lot of principals don't utilize lesson plans with their staff is because they're confused as to what an effective lesson plan looks like, or they don't understand the plan's value as a communication tool and fail to invest the time in really reviewing it. A system in which teachers are required to turn in lesson plans to their administration for review only works when the administration takes the time to instruct staff as to what effective plans look like and then follows up with legitimate comments and feedback for each set of plans. Does this mean that you have to write what you thought on every lesson plan? No. Does this mean you'll have to read every lesson plan? Yes, you will for a while. You'll also need to review regularly the lesson plans from all new teachers and those teachers you have concerns about.

What are the parts of an effective lesson plan?

The nice thing about lesson plans is that you can tailor the format for your school. If your district requires a particular format, don't assume that's all your school will need. You may want to add other opportunities for your staff to explain what they're doing in their classrooms that relate to specific goals at your school.

Lesson plans vary with each school district; however, below is a list of the standard components of what most lesson plans should include and brief definitions of these components.

OBJECTIVE

The objective is what the teacher wants the students to be able to do by the end of the lesson. An effective formula for writing objectives includes a statement about students being able to physically demonstrate an understanding of a concept, for example: *Students will be able to identify four words that begin with the letter* K *by naming objects displayed by the teacher that begin with the letter* K. Another example might be the following: *Students will be able to add four sight words to their literacy repertoire by identifying them on a list.*

MATERIALS

This is the opportunity for the teacher to explain to you which materials and tools he or she will be using in class. This doesn't mean that the teacher must use new-fangled gadgets—chalk and paper are acceptable materials in many creative contexts.

OPENING SET

This is the where the teacher begins to explain how the lesson will be taught. The opening set is the very first thing he or she does to catch the students' attention and to make them think. The opening set only needs to be a couple of sentences. As all newly trained teachers, curriculum specialists, and philosophers like John Dewey would argue, this is also the place for the teacher to do something to weave the lesson into students' prior knowledge. For example, a teacher whose objective is to have students write a descriptive paragraph, might plan the opening set in the following way:

> I plan to ask my students to close their eyes and think of a time
> when they felt so angry that they could feel their hearts beating.
> Next I'll have them open their eyes and tell me about what made

The Principal's Essential Guide to Literacy in the Elementary School them so angry. Then I'll talk about the book that we are about to read, which is about an angry young man. I'll hold up the cover of the book and ask the students to try and guess, based on the cover art work, why the protagonist of the book is so angry. I'll ask them to keep track of descriptive words and phrases that would be useful in a paragraph about a time they were very angry.

METHOD OF DELIVERY

It's here that you'll find most teachers writing phrases such as *group discussion, small-group activities, think-pair-share, scavenger hunts, experiments, computer research*, and *guest speakers*. Be wary of these phrases. Often teachers throw in whatever they can think of because it's hard for them to describe to you what they'll be doing. Don't feel intimidated because a teacher includes some technical terms here that you might not be familiar with. It might mean that they really don't have a grasp of what they're doing, or it might mean that they're using a technique that you don't feel is valuable. For example, if you find out that *popcorn reading* is a time in which one child reads one sentence and then another child reads the following sentence and so forth, you might want to witness this in class yourself to gauge its effectiveness. Talk to the teacher about how often students engage in this activity, how valuable it is for them, and what the teacher bases this evaluation upon. You might discover that popcorn reading steals opportunities for students to practice their fluency, their ability to read smoothly, because they're focused on who's reading next and they're having to start abruptly and then stop at the end of a sentence.

ASSESSMENT

Perhaps the most important part of a lesson plan is assessment. Authentic assessment is when the teacher requires each individual student to do something physically measurable that demonstrates his or her understanding of an objective. Often teachers think they're engaged in "authentic teaching." Authentic teaching means that teachers are really delivering something valuable and relevant to students' minds. The discussions among politicians and educators concerning what is valuable and relevant have fueled national controversies and state-level legislation concerning standardized tests. (For a more in-depth look at this issue, read *The Manufactured Crisis* by David Berliner and Bruce Biddle.) For the purposes of this discussion, principals need to be mindful that teachers often truly believe they're delivering a legitimate lesson. Unfortunately, it can be tempting to forget what is age-appropriate and valuable in a classroom.

The example curriculum experts often use to explain how one can confuse an authentic lesson with an engaging lesson is cooking in class. Students making holiday cookies in a fifth-grade homeroom class because it's the last week of school before the holiday break is not an authentic lesson. The lesson would gain authenticity if the fifth graders had just finished reading a book about the history of cookies and were studying the science and math of measurement.

Planning a lesson in which one group of students measures the ingredients in a cookie recipe accurately and bakes them while another group doesn't measure the ingredients accurately makes sense. The two groups can then taste the cookies and compare the differences between the two batches. Then they could write a paragraph about what they learned about the importance of measurement that could be posted on a bulletin board in the classroom. The teacher would then make an assessment of the lesson by reviewing the students' paragraphs.

ALIGNMENT TO STATE STANDARDS

In this section, the teacher can communicate to the principal as well as to the community what students are doing in class that relates to the educational grade-level standards set by the state. What's nice about this part of a lesson plan is that teachers must think about their teaching in general and in specific ways and decide how the lesson relates to the mandated educational standards. This also empowers teachers to actually read the standards. A typical example in this section might include the following: *This lesson meets educational grade-level writing standard 3.1 ["The students use adjectives effectively in writing"]; writing standard 3.4 ["The students use proper punctuation when crafting sentences"]; and reading standard 5.1 ["Students are able to identify the central plot and protagonist of a story"] of the state standards for grade 5.* Again, this section provides a wonderful opportunity to discuss the state- and district-level expectations for the school with your staff at a faculty meeting. It also allows you to demonstrate to your governing board that your staff aligns curriculum to state standards, as evidenced by your teachers' lesson plans.

EXPECTATIONS

This section is the place for your teachers to communicate what they're doing to meet your global expectations. Remember the chart you made earlier for classroom goals, community goals, and struggling readers? The expectations section can be divided into these three areas for the teacher to share his or her own goals.

A simple way to ensure that teachers stay focused on these expectations is to create a lesson plan form yourself. Include the sections mentioned above, and allow space for a teacher to insert his or her information. Although you can e-mail these forms to teachers so they can complete them on the computers, make sure you also have hard copies available as some teachers may prefer to complete them by hand.

What do you look for when you review a lesson plan?

One of the biggest mistakes that principals make is to require lesson plans from their teachers without ever reading them. Invest in maintaining your high level of credibility as an instructional leader by taking the time to review lesson plans and make comments on these documents before returning them to your teachers. Lesson planning is the most important part of the teacher evaluation process as it is the arena where you and your faculty have the chance to talk to each other, regularly and consistently, about the specifics of delivering instruction. When you review teachers' lesson plans, check that the assessment matches the objective. Authentic assessment of a student's learning should happen at the end of the lesson. It's not appropriate or accurate for students to be assessed by questions the teacher asks the entire class. Since one or two students may answer the questions, how does the teacher know that everyone has achieved the objective? The most desirable assessment usually involves students writing something individually such as a reflective paragraph or sentence. In turn, the teacher reviews the written work and returns quick comments back to students. The students' reflections also help the teacher monitor and adjust instruction. If a student "didn't get it," the teacher needs to reteach the lesson again the next day.

Another thing to look for in a lesson plan is the variety of methods a teacher uses. Does the teacher change his or her approach, or is this a monotonous class for students? Finally, consider if the objective is age- and grade-level appropriate. If you think the answer is no, ask the teacher to explain the appropriateness of the objective. After you review the lesson plan and make notes to yourself, decide on three things to focus on when you have your pre-observation conference with the teacher.

THE PRE-OBSERVATION CONFERENCE

It's a very good idea to hold a faculty meeting to explain what a pre-observation conference will be like. The purpose of a pre-observation conference is not only to understand how the teacher utilizes his or her lesson plans; it is also a chance to ask the teacher how you can best provide support when you come to visit the classroom and evaluate his or her teaching skills. At this meeting, again remind the staff of your expectations and review what you look for in a lesson plan. If you share evaluation duties with an administrative colleague and you have established whom you'll be evaluating, make sure to send out memos to your staff as soon as possible informing them of the date and time they'll be meeting with you. If you are charged with all the teacher evaluations in your building, make sure you are as timely as possible in notifying teachers of the date and time you would like to meet for a pre-observation conference.

When you start the pre-observation conference, make sure that you and the teacher are sitting at a table together or in a nonthreatening place—and that you're not sitting across from each other at a desk. After welcoming the teacher, explain that you reviewed the lesson plan and ask him or her to go over it with you. Ask questions during this discussion. Before approaching your concerns, always affirm the teacher first with at least two positive comments about the plan. Most teachers forget the affirmations and concentrate only on the concerns, so make sure you lower the level of threat a teacher may feel by affirming the strengths you see. If you can, weave some positive statements about what you've already seen in his or her classroom and then ask if the teacher would like you to look for something in particular to give feedback on. Sometimes teachers, like the new principal mentioned at the beginning of this chapter, may try to impress you with vocabulary or statements about their intent that only serves to demonstrate that they don't know what they're talking about.

Given below are a few hints to help you figure out if your pre-observation conference is really an attempt by a teacher to fool you into thinking that he or she is an expert. For example, a teacher might be exaggerating an understanding of pedagogy when he or she does the following:

* Offers a rambling answer when you ask specific questions about the reason behind a specific instructional approach

* Is unwilling (or unable) to reflect with any depth when asked to explain certain choices in planning

* Appears to "string" the same sorts adjectives and jargon over and over when asked to describe what he or she is doing instead of giving a more in-depth answer

THE OBSERVATION

The most important thing to remember concerning an observation visit to a classroom is the seriousness of the event. It doesn't matter how jaded or confident the teacher appears; this is the moment to demonstrate expertise to his or her supervisor. Most teachers are nervous because they want everything to be perfect.

An unspoken practice that principals use to navigate through a too busy day is to be late to meetings or to leave meetings early, because they can. After all, they are the bosses. However, we strongly advise you to suspend this managerial trick when it comes to classroom visits. Honor the sanctity of your role as the curriculum leader and be on time for an observation. This is one meeting that you cannot afford to be late for. Your actions during the visit quickly educate your staff about who you are as a leader. It's here where you need to pay particular attention to front-stage behavior. Many principals make the mistake of thinking that just because they've told a teacher that he or she is terrific and that they intend to give a good evaluation, they can exert minimal effort for the observation. If you do this, you will lose credibility with your staff. Even the excellent teachers who you assumed gave you their loyalty will crucify you in the lounge because you didn't give them the professional respect they deserve by thoughtfully engaging in their evaluations.

When the time for the observation arrives, take a legal pad on a clipboard and a pen with you to the classroom. Also carry a watch so you can see the time clearly. When you enter the classroom, a teacher may ask you where you want to sit. Choose a seat in the back, and try to make your entry as nonintrusive as possible. Observation visits are the time for you to be invisible and carefully watch what is going on.

There are myriad ways to actually script or record a lesson that you observe. Your district may have a system that you're required to follow. If not, a simple way to script is to draw a line down the left side of your paper. Use that section of the paper to note each time that the teacher moves to the next section of the lesson. This is called the *transition*. The most desirable lessons have relatively short opening sets and a short closure. The lengthiest part of the lesson should be the delivery of instruction. By noting the transition times, you'll be able to roughly gauge if the teacher stays focused on the pace of the lesson and includes each part of the lesson plan within the time allowed for it.

Utilize the section to the right of the line for time notations to follow your lesson plan format. You can make notes related to these sections (i.e., set, delivery, assessment, and expectations) as they occur during the lesson. You may want to note whether the teacher walked around the classroom, which students were called on, and if the class remained engaged.

Consider the following items when you observe and script a lesson:

* Write the teacher's name, date, class, and time in the upper right-hand corner of the page.

* Draw a margin on the left side of your writing pad, and use it to note the time at various intervals. For example, when the lesson begins, note the time.

* After you've recorded the first notation of time, write down a description of what you see on the chalkboard.

* Next, write down what the teacher is doing for the opening set.

* When the set is finished and the teacher is moving on to something else, write down the time in the left margin. Effective teachers at any grade level have regular and consistent transitions.

* Write down when students ask questions.

* Note who the teacher questions; write down the names of the students.

* Write down the type of method used: small group, partners, and so on.

* Because there are so many things on a principal's mind, it can be hard to really focus on the task of evaluating the lesson you are observing. When it gets a little difficult for you to concentrate, write down in the right margin how the classroom is decorated. Is current student work posted? Is there a sense of theme and order in the classroom environment?

* Write down what kind of discipline you see. Does the teacher maintain an orderly classroom environment?

* Note when you see students off task. Include their names if possible and the exact time you observed this.

* Record the time when you see the closing activity.

* Note the kind of assessment the teacher used.

How do you analyze your scripting notes from a classroom observation?

Principals typically analyze their script notes when they have a moment to concentrate and fill out the teacher evaluation document. That moment is usually hours or days after the observation. Writing quick notes about general observations when you leave a classroom allows you to archive details that you might forget without a moment's reflection. So, after you leave the classroom with your scripted notes, take two minutes (even if it's on the sidewalk outside the classroom) to write down any additional comments about your visit such the rapport you saw between students and teacher. Also jot down any questions you have for the teacher such as *Why did you select this method to deliver the lesson?*

The following list of global questions will help you with a scripting analysis. (They're also relevant to all evaluation instruments.)

* Were all the parts of a minimal lesson covered: opening set, delivery of instruction, and assessment?

* Was there closure for the lesson? In other words, was the teacher able to restate what was learned in class?

* Did the actual lesson match the lesson plan?

* What were the transition times? Was there an even flow? Was too much time spent on one activity, thus throwing off balance in the lesson?

* Was this an authentic lesson versus a lesson that was only entertaining?

* Was the assessment authentic?

* What did this lesson have to do with state standards?

* What kind of questioning strategies were used? Were all the questions knowledge level, or were there more complicated analysis and synthesis questions?

* Did the teacher only call on girls or only call on boys?

* Did the teacher call on anyone sitting in the back of the room?

* Did the teacher treat students with dignity?

* Did the students treat the teacher with respect?

* What did the classroom feel like? Was it inviting?

* Was student work displayed?

* Did the teacher connect with the students? Were the students engaged and on task?

* Was the teacher passionate about the subject matter?

* Was the teacher able to empower students to connect the lesson to the real world?

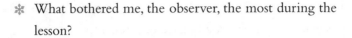

* What bothered me, the observer, the most during the lesson?

* What did I like the most during the lesson?

* Was there a sense of discipline and order in the class?

How do you prepare for a post-observation conference?

Once you've analyzed your notes, prepare for the post-observation conference by choosing three things you saw during your visit to praise the teacher for and one suggestion for his or her growth. This can be difficult as sometimes there are five things that a teacher should focus on. For purposes of the post-observation discussion, a ratio of three positives to one challenge is appropriate. If your scripting reveals too many inadequacies in the classroom, you may want to consider putting the teacher on a plan of improvement or even moving to non-renew that teacher.

Fill out the district evaluation instrument, and don't be afraid to write suggestions for improvement in the comments section. Use the phrase, *Continue to focus on…*, when writing a challenge. This verbiage softens the language and eases the reader into reflecting on what you're saying. As for the positives, start compliments with phrases such as *Mr. Jones is a great addition to our staff. His strengths include…*

Be aware of what happens when you give teachers all perfect scores on their evaluations. If you choose not to give a suggestion for improvement, you're telling your staff that they don't need to improve on anything, which contributes to a false sense of perfection among your teaching staff. As a consequence, you may have teachers coming to you to complain that they got a four instead of a perfect five score for bulletin boards. As a culture, we educators often find it difficult to reflect legitimately upon our strengths and weaknesses. By perpetuating the myth of perfection in your staff, you perpetuate mediocrity and a lack of self-reflection. Ultimately, this affects the quality of experiences that your students receive.

How do you conduct a post-observation conference?

When you meet with the teacher to discuss the classroom observation, remember that it is really important to demonstrate that you value him or her by being on time and prepared for the meeting. Know that the teacher will be nervous. Start the conference in a neutral spot in your office; again, do not have your teacher sit on one side of your desk and you on the other. Begin the conference by asking the teacher how he or she thought the lesson went. Be quiet and let the teacher talk. If he or she says only that is was fine, respond by asking, *What about the lesson was fine?* Use other probing questions such as *Tell me more about that...* to help the teacher really reflect on what happened in the classroom. As appropriate, interject statements concerning the strengths you saw.

In most cases, the teacher will identify the challenges or weaknesses that you observed in the classroom. For example, suppose the script notes for Mr. Jones's class revealed that there was no assessment of student learning and that there were 20 minutes of group work. A question also arose as to how the objective was related to the state standards for fourth graders. There was also a note concerning how his classroom looked. If Mr. Jones were in a post-observation conference with his principal, it might go something like the following:

PRINCIPAL: How do you think the lesson went?

JONES: I felt like time got away from us. The kids were just so excited about the Canfield Fair this weekend. Everything in *Charlotte's Web* is about the animals, and it seemed like we focused on Wilbur the pig today and the Canfield Fair rather than what was happening to Charlotte in the book. Before I knew it, the bell had rung.

PRINCIPAL: Yes, I saw that. But it was also clear that you're passionate about this book and making it real for your students. Since a lot of them come from families that work on farms, it made sense that they were interested in what you were saying. Tell me about Darius. He's quite a card.

JONES: Yeah, I saw him passing notes, but I didn't want to interrupt the flow of the discussion.

PRINCIPAL: Is there a way you could have kept Darius on task?

JONES: Well, I guess I could have stopped the entire class to reprimand him. I just didn't want to waste class time.

PRINCIPAL: I see your point. Tell me more about wasting class time. Where is it that you think the clock got away from you?

JONES: Well…we spent a lot of time on the kind of farms there are in Canfield.

PRINCIPAL: I wonder what would have happened if you had given students five minutes to talk about the kinds of farms in our neighborhood, instead of ten minutes.

JONES: Maybe that would have made a difference.

PRINCIPAL: I also wanted to mention that it's clear the kids like you and enjoy your class. I think your student rapport is definitely a strength. I liked the movie posters on your walls. You have some student projects displayed from last semester. Is there any way you can balance that by putting up some student essays that are more current? One of the purposes of displaying student work is to reinforce the fact that they're doing a great job, and you want to do that regularly. That's why keeping your displays current is so important. I know you know all of this, but there's so much to remember in a classroom.

JONES: Yes, you're right. There are a million things to remember. Normally my student work is current. I think you caught me on a bad day, but yes, I can update the bulletin board.

PRINCIPAL: You know, I also like the fact that you're getting our kids to see how real life is found in literature. I thought your objective of teaching sympathy and empathy was an interesting one, and it matched your lesson plan. And using *Charlotte's Web* is a great idea for this lesson. However, because your transition time was a little sluggish, you didn't have time to assess whether your students learned anything about the concepts of empathy and sympathy. There is one thing I would encourage you to do: Watch those transitions so you can actually assess whether your students met your objective. I also want to reiterate again that your students love coming to your class. I know you do a great deal of extra-curricular work for our school with your coaching, too.

It's a real pleasure to work with you. If you look at the evaluation instrument I've given you, you can see your scores in these areas. In the comments section, I've written that you're a team-oriented colleague, that you're popular with our students, and that you're passionate about the subject you teach. You can also see that I've encouraged you to be conscious of your transition times to ensure that there's an opportunity for you to assess whether your students met the objective of your lesson. Are there any questions I can answer for you?

JONES: No, not at the moment.

PRINCIPAL: If you think of any, please let me know. I need you to sign this form to show that you've received your evaluation. I'm glad we got a chance to talk. Thanks for coming in.

What the dialogue above demonstrates is that the evaluation instrument presents only one point of reflection. The principal selected the one point of reflection to write down by going back to the list of expectations about teaching that he'd created for himself. However, during the conference, the principal raised several things for the teacher to think about. This principal knows that curriculum leadership requires more than checking what's written on the chalkboard.

Summary

The evaluation of instruction is not only a skill set, but an art that many school administrators invest an entire career in perfecting. And like other aspects of leadership, evaluating instruction is both context-specific and related to the professional compass that changes in small ways with the politics of education at local, state, and federal levels. What we presented in this chapter was a basic scaffold to help you begin your own litany of understanding concerning how one helps a teacher reflect on instructional delivery practices, celebrate strengths in the classroom, and set (as well as meet) new goals as a teacher. We all agree that the one thing girding this whole process is a commitment to valuing your teachers by offering them the utmost respect via your time, preparation, and sincere attention to their efforts.

CHAPTER 5

How Can Your Team Support Different Kinds of Learners?

Mr. Stithson, the principal of Jackson Elementary School, had a problem. Results from the annual statewide literacy assessment indicated that students in his school were not performing up to par. The number of students reading at a proficient level or better was below state and local norms. Moreover, the percentage of students achieving below the proficient level had actually increased over the past three years, while across the state and in his school district, the trend was decidedly toward a decrease in performance below expectations. Mr. Stithson recognized that his school was located in an inner-city area with high levels of poverty and a significant number of students who came from different ethnic backgrounds and for whom English was not the first language. However, he also recognized that these factors couldn't be used as an excuse for students' poor performance. All students were expected to perform up to grade level or better.

It was May, and Mr. Stithson was thinking about the next school year. Something had to be done to improve the reading performance of those students who weren't performing at a proficient level. He called a meeting of his faculty and explained the situation. The school needed to plan now to help students who were not succeeding in reading and in other subjects.

The scenario described in the preceding paragraphs is not new. Schools around the country are being forced now more than ever to confront the reality that significant numbers of their students are not proficient in reading. Although home and environmental circumstances are most definitely factors in student performance, we can no longer ascribe poor performance to those factors. Schools are agents for change in society; in their most ideal sense, they lift students out of poverty and point them toward a better life for themselves and their communities. Literacy is a key to both the lifting and living a better life. Thus, if we want our schools to realize this ideal for the most students, we must confront the problems of our students who don't achieve the expectations we have for them in literacy. We must embrace our students who pose particular challenges in literacy instruction.

In this chapter, we deal with questions related to struggling readers, gifted readers, and how you can best support their teachers. Here is a brief outline of specific questions we will be addressing:

* Which students in my school are different in terms of their reading achievement? How are they identified?

* How do we determine and monitor their progress in reading?

* How do we, as a school community, help students who are different?

Which students in your school are struggling in reading?

There are many ways in which students in our schools differ from each other. They differ in size. They differ by gender. They have different interests. Students' social and economic circumstances differ. Many of our students come from impoverished economic environments. The makeup of their families differs. Very few families today consist of the stereotypical two parents, two kids, a dog, and a cat. In some families, both parents live at home. In other cases, grandparents are the primary custodians of their grandchildren. Foster families are also common. Our students come from many kinds of families and many kinds of environments. They also differ in their cultural, ethnic, or linguistic backgrounds. The United States and Canada have always been countries of immigrants, so it's no surprise that nearly all our schools are filled with students who come from a variety of ethnic and cultural backgrounds. Moreover, in some schools, a multitude of languages are spoken. To complicate matters further, many of these languages use writing systems and symbols that are markedly different from those we use in English.

Needless to say, the students you see in your school can and do differ in a variety of important conditions. Many of the dimensions described above, as well as others, can have an impact on students' levels of achievement in reading. However, despite their association with reading achievement, there is often little we can do to influence these conditions. We cannot by ourselves easily improve the economic circumstances of our students or their families. We certainly don't want to try to alter anyone's cultural background—indeed, we should demonstrate respect for all the cultures represented in our schools. We should focus our limited energies on those things over which we do have some degree of responsibility and control.

Thus, we need to be interested in students who differ in reading achievement—those whose progress are below what we expect, as well as those whose are significantly above norm. We need to focus on the factors that contribute to that difference, especially if it contributes negatively to students' reading achievement. These contributory factors in reading include those identified by the National Reading Panel (2000) and described in Chapter 2 such as difficulties in phonemic awareness, phonics and decoding, reading fluency, vocabulary, and comprehension. Other factors may be a lack of motivation for reading and a lack of volume of reading material.

How can you identify these students?

Since we're concerned with reading achievement, we need to limit the discussion to those reading-related factors that affect reading achievement and that we can control to some degree. You shouldn't allow yourself to over-complicate the matter by bringing in and trying to deal with factors that you cannot change—gender, economic circumstances, cultural and linguistic background, and so on. These are important factors and need to be part of the overall discussion. However, it is fruitless and can be counterproductive to use them to identify students with reading problems and to attempt to alter them. For instance, trying to make students (and their families) more American by emphasizing English and American culture while dismissing or denigrating their native culture is likely to alienate them.

Identifying students' academic performance in reading is straightforward and simple. And, as discussed previously, your school should have a reading assessment, diagnosis, and progress monitoring policy in place.

The first line of identification is your teachers. They're the ones who will first notice when a student is not "getting it," so it is important that teachers get the appropriate training in identifying and working with these students. Of equal importance is setting procedures for teachers to communicate their findings to you or someone in the school, perhaps the school literacy coordinator, who can provide further assessment of the identified students and record the results into a control log that allows you and other school personnel to easily identify the students and to monitor their progress.

A second method for identification is testing–standardized testing or less formal but equally valid screening for reading problems. Standardized reading tests have been around for a long time, and many schools and school districts have a regular regimen for administering them to students at the beginning or end of the school year. Although a lot of money, time, and effort were put into purchasing and administering the tests, the problem in the past has been that little was ever done with the results. Results were normally sent home to parents, and the school reports were often filed away in the principal's office. In our experience, it's not uncommon for a school to have these results piled in cardboard boxes sitting on the floor of the principal's office—inaccessible to anyone who might want to know how individual children performed. What a waste!

If resources, time, and energy are going to be spent on such an effort, then something should be done with the results. Certainly, it's important for parents to be notified of their children's test performance. Equally important, however, is the need to use the results to identify students who aren't performing as expected–those whose reading, for whatever reason, is significantly below grade level or other expectations. This can be your task, but it can also be done by the school literacy coordinator, or by individual teachers.

Most states have mandated the annual testing of students, at least at certain grade levels. These state-mandated proficiency tests in reading, meant to show the progress that schools and school districts are making in teaching reading, also can easily be used to initially screen students who aren't performing up to standards or expectations in reading.

More informal screening devices can also be used to identify those students at risk. Informal reading inventories (IRI) have been used for this purpose for decades. However, the major drawback to informal reading inventories and similar tests is time–they simply take too much time to administer to a group of students. Not counting scoring and interpretation, each IRI can take up to an hour to administer. It can take up to 20 hours to administer an IRI to a classroom of 20 students–that's four full days of school given over to testing! Moreover, in some schools, teachers are required to administer IRIs three or more times a year to demonstrate that students are making adequate progress. Thus, a full complement of IRI testing could rob students and teachers of up to 60 hours of school, hours that could have been devoted more effectively to focused instruction and authentic reading. Time given over to assessment is time taken away from instruction.

We need screening instruments in reading that are quick and easy and valid. This recognition led Tim Rasinski and Nancy Padak (2005) to develop their *Three-Minute Reading Assessment* books. In these books, Padak and Rasinski explain how teachers can utilize a three-minute reading assessment instrument and gain an understanding of their students' reading level. Their approach to reading assessment involves students in reading one passage; from that passage, teachers can gain a sense of whether students are performing at grade level in reading comprehension, fluency, and word decoding. Other quick and effective screening devices such as DIBELS (Dynamic Indicators of Basic Early Literacy) are also available.

The outcome of this testing, whatever approach and method you and your school use, is to identify those students who are different: Identify those students who score well above expectations, and most especially, those students who perform well below expectations. Students identified as different need to be logged into some control system so that their progress in reading can be monitored more closely. This could be a logbook in which names and appropriate data are entered; it could be a computerized spreadsheet.

The poor-performing students need the best instruction that meets their needs. In fact, they need more instruction if we expect to see them make progress in reading. Once we identify these students, we can develop a system for controlling and monitoring their progress as they receive instruction.

DIAGNOSING DIFFERENCES

Identifying a student's difference is not enough. Many students may not be performing up to snuff in reading, but they're likely to be doing so for different reasons. The next step is diagnosing the cause of their reading difficulties. While we can identify poverty, linguistic and cultural differences, gender, and the like as causes of reading problems, these are challenges we can do little about. We must look deeper and more particularly at the reading factors that are likely to be at the root of the identified reading problem.

Thus, for the limited number of students who aren't performing at an appropriate level in reading, diagnostic assessment is called for. Diagnostic assessment is a more involved set of assessments designed to identify the specific components of a student's reading problem. We should be looking specifically at those components of reading identified by the National Reading Panel (2000)–phonemic awareness, phonics, fluency, vocabulary, and comprehension–as well as other factors associated specifically with reading such as volume of reading at home and in school, sight word recognition, spelling, attitude toward reading, and reading interests.

Diagnostic assessment is normally administered by a trained specialist in reading. In your school, this may be the reading coach or reading specialist or the classroom teacher who has had such training. The types of diagnostic assessments can range from formal, commercially developed assessments that require a precise and rule-governed administration (in order to compare each student's performance against norms that have been developed by the preparer of the test) to more informal diagnostic assessments that rely more on authentic reading tasks that are observed carefully by the reading specialist. The informal measures rely more heavily on the training and expertise of the tester to make inferences about the student's reading behaviors and their nature and cause. We think a combination of diagnostic assessments is best as they combine carefully developed standards of student performance with the expertise of your professional staff who are well aware of the background of individual students and the general milieu of the school and the community.

Although we don't advocate any particular assessment, we think that the best diagnostic assessment instruments are IRIs which, as mentioned earlier in this chapter, involve students reading words and passages of various difficulty that mirror the kinds of passages they read in school and then having them respond to the passages either by answering questions about content or by a retelling of the passages. Any reading specialist worth his or her salt should be very familiar with the nature and protocols involved in the administration of an IRI. Moreover, we recommend that you ask your reading specialist to include the IRI or elements of it in the reading diagnostic protocol.

However, diagnostic testing can be problematic. It provides teachers with excellent information about helping students become better readers, and that's a good thing. However, when principals recognize the value of this information, they may want to have all students tested diagnostically. We've seen schools implement a policy that *all* students be tested diagnostically every year. In most extreme cases, students are tested diagnostically two or three times a year. While we can certainly sympathize with the reasoning behind such policies, we also recognize a significant concern. All testing takes time, but diagnostic testing takes a lot of time. Again, time given to testing is time taken away from instruction. What we've seen happening in some schools is that so much time is given to testing students that little time is given to teaching, so, periodic testing may not show as much progress as you'd like or would expect to see. Please avoid the pitfall of mandating that all students be administered a diagnostic assessment. Not all students need it. Those who appear to be reading at grade level and who are making appropriate progress in reading, as determined by screening assessments, don't need further diagnostic testing. The information gained from the diagnostic assessment won't be very helpful for altering or steering their instruction. If screening tests determine that students are making good progress in reading, the instructional inference to teachers is simple—keep doing what you've been doing with these students because it seems to be working!

Diagnostic assessment should provide reading-related information that the classroom teacher and intervention teacher (if assigned to work with the student) can use to improve the student's reading performance. The reading specialist should develop a report for each diagnostic assessment that, at a minimum, summarizes screening and diagnostic assessments and provides doable recommendations that teachers can use to help a student maximize growth in reading. Parents should be informed of the results, consulted about their own insights into the student's reading problem, and provided with recommendations to help their child at home. The report should be filed in the student's personal school record. Finally, the results also should be summarized in short form, perhaps on a spreadsheet, so that both you and the school reading specialist have easy access for monitoring.

How do you teach students who struggle in reading?

Identifying, diagnosing, and monitoring the progress of students who struggle in reading and their specific areas of concern is only half the problem. Once you and your faculty know something about these students, the next question is: *What will you do to help them improve their reading?* Clearly, screening and diagnostic assessment have little value unless the information and recommendations gleaned from such assessments are put to use. As the instructional leader for your school, you need to take the guiding role in ensuring that an intervention program for struggling readers is developed.

The first step is to get the entire faculty on board with reading intervention. The faculty, or a faculty committee with you as a member, should develop a reading intervention plan or policy for your school. This begins with a statement of mission and principles for helping struggling readers. The mission statement will be the framework to guide your school's work with struggling readers. It should be flexible enough to meet individual student and teacher needs, yet rigorous enough to ensure that each and every student is provided with the best possible instruction.

We believe the following principles should be included in your mission statement:

Individualized instruction: Instructional plans for students who struggle should address the specific needs identified in the diagnostic assessment. Moreover, the mission statement should identify the teachers who have the primary instructional responsibility. These will usually be the classroom teacher or the reading intervention teacher. Other teachers who may influence the student's reading instruction (music, art, physical education) may also be included.

Instructional level: Your reading intervention plan needs to identify each struggling reader's reading level and strive to match his or her reading and reading instruction to the appropriate level. Struggling readers don't read much when they're given the opportunity because the material they choose (or that's assigned to them) is often too difficult for them. Your program and plan need to work toward making a good match between text and activity difficulty and a student's current level of reading performance.

Appropriate grouping: Individualizing instruction also means addressing the number of students who are to receive instruction at a given time. Ideally, instruction for struggling readers should be individualized. Logistically, this may not be possible, so decisions need to be made about the appropriate size of the instructional group for each struggling reader—individual, paired instruction, small group, larger group, homogeneous or heterogeneous group, or some combination.

Maximizing time for instruction: The amount of instructional time is strongly correlated to progress in reading. Thus, planning for students with reading difficulties should attempt to maximize instructional time. This may include regular classroom instruction time, small-group targeted instruction time, time for individual or small-group tutoring from the intervention teacher, or some combination.

Maximizing time for authentic reading: We know a correlation exists between the amount of real reading done by students and their progress in reading (Allington, 2002). Instructional plans for students should attempt to maximize the amount of reading they do–in school, at home, during vacations, and so on. Moreover, since struggling readers often don't read as much as they could when given the opportunity, your plan should include provisions for making students accountable for their authentic reading. This may mean asking them to keep a journal of the time they spend reading or to give oral summaries of their reading to a teacher or other responsible adult.

Parental/home involvement: Any effective instructional program needs to extend the instructional experience beyond the school and into the home (see Chapter 8) and the community (see Chapter 9). In particular, involving parents and other immediate family members of struggling readers can have a profoundly positive effect on their reading development, so home involvement is a must when planning for students with reading difficulties. Involvement can include effective two-way communication, parents monitoring their children's reading activities, and active instruction by parents. The reading specialist and reading teachers should be able to tailor specific home activities that can provide the greatest assistance to students.

Materials for instruction: The planning document for helping struggling readers must provide a wide range of appropriate materials for students, and mostly certainly should include authentic literature that represents a variety of reading levels, genres, and interests/topics. Again, if we want students to read, we need to provide them with as many opportunities for real reading as possible.

At the same time, planning must include specific instructional programs and materials for struggling readers. Programs such as Reading Recovery and Early Intervention in Reading (EIR), along with their accompanying materials, need to be considered. If such programs are appropriate and desirable for your school, you will need to allocate resources needed to obtain and support them.

Develop instructional routines: Instruction that will have the greatest impact on struggling readers is not merely a collection of related methods and materials. Rather, it's a thoughtfully planned set or series of instructional activities, all related to some aspect of the learner's literacy needs and development, which are delivered on a regular schedule. In other words, the mission statement you develop for your school should state that the faculty is dedicated to developing and implementing integrated instructional routines for students who struggle in learning to read. The routines should be based on students' instructional needs and on the faculty's understanding of effective reading instruction. Additionally, since an instructional routine is a regular and predictable set of activities for students and teachers, the explanation for each activity is kept to a minimum. Time is most effectively and efficiently employed in the activity itself.

Most effective programs for working with struggling readers include some type of routine. For example, in Reading Recovery, each 30-minute lesson consists of a series of instructional activities that are delivered daily and largely in the same order. They include introducing and reading a new leveled book each day; reading a previously read book; sentence writing; and letter, sound, and word work.

If a teacher chooses not to rely on an existing program or routine for a particular student, an instructional plan should nevertheless be developed and implemented as a routine, with each component aimed at a specific instructional need of the student.

How do you put principles guiding reading intervention into action?

Once the principles that will guide reading intervention services have been agreed upon, you and your faculty should establish a protocol or set of procedures to guide the process of helping students who are behind in their reading development. Key issues that need to be addressed here include the following:

* Who will be responsible for guiding the intervention program in your school? Will there be one leader or an intervention team that guides and supports the program? If there will be a team, who will be on it and when will they meet?

* How will students be identified, and how will they be placed into the appropriate level of intervention services? Assessment will certainly be used in the identification process, but will identification occur only

at certain times of the year, or will there be an ongoing program of identification? Who will make the determination of the appropriate level of intervention: an individual person or a team?

* How will parents be involved in the intervention program? Will they be asked to take an active role? If so, what will that role be? Or will they simply be informed of what's happening to their children at school? Who will be responsible for parental communication?

* How will students' progress be monitored? How will they exit the program? What records will be kept, and how will they be maintained?

These questions, and any others you have, should be asked and answered before the school year begins. No one set of answers will work for every school. Each school is different in the same way that each student is different. Thus, just as the needs of each student must be considered when providing instruction, the needs of each individual school must be considered when developing policies and plans that will most effectively guide its work with students.

The process of accommodating the needs of students who struggle to read can be quite complicated, but it's essential that you establish a system that will work for you, your faculty, and—most especially—for your students. They need the very best that we can give them. We must provide students with the best instruction, but we also have to develop a system that allows you and your faculty to identify struggling students as early as possible, to intervene as intensively as necessary, and to know when to allow them to exit so that other students who also need intervention can take advantage of our limited resources.

How do you teach gifted readers?

Another area of exceptionality or difference concerns students who are gifted in reading. Shouldn't they also receive a form of differentiated instruction? This is really a tough question to answer. On the surface, it seems that the answer should be in the affirmative. Students who are gifted in one or more areas certainly deserve opportunities to nurture their talent.

The thing to keep in mind, however, is that reading is not a specific content area or special area of knowledge to be learned; it's a tool for accessing other domains of knowledge. Thus, it seems to us that if students are gifted in reading, they're most likely gifted in other areas. If they're enrolled in programs for gifted and talented students, it's likely that they'll have the opportunity to engage in reading activities and materials that will stretch that talent. These students will automatically have opportunities for using the very skills that have helped them achieve so well.

On the other hand, we feel that all students possess gifts and talents, and every student needs the opportunity to engage in the deep, thoughtful, and varied reading that's often reserved for those students who have been specifically identified by testing or teacher nomination for special instruction. How can a school offer such experiences to all students? One way is through extracurricular activities that involve deep reading, in-depth discussion, and elaborated response. Book or reading clubs, open to all students, that extend beyond the regular classroom and school day provide such opportunities.

As the principal, you have the unique opportunity to model such a program for your staff, parents, and other volunteers who want to become involved. Reserve a part of your day for reading with students by beginning a Principal's Reading Club that meets each week before, during, or after the school day.

In consultation with your teachers, choose a book of high literary quality and varied genre (biography, novel, poetry, mystery, and so on) for the club members to read over the course of several weeks. Invite students from targeted grade levels to enroll in your club. Then meet for 30 to 45 minutes each week to discuss the section of the book that you assigned at the last meeting. Engage in the type of deep and varied discussions that are found in adult book clubs; model for your teachers the types of discussion you'd like to see in their classrooms; and of course, empathize with them in the trials and tribulations of getting discussions off the ground.

Your teachers will love you for this! So will parents! So will students! When everyone finishes the book, plan a response activity to engage you and the students in a task that will deepen their understanding of and appreciation for the book. Examples of these response activities include the following: writing letters to government officials after reading a book with an environmental theme; visiting a historic site, museum, or another location after reading about it; bringing in a guest speaker (perhaps a knowledgeable parent) who can elaborate on the topic of the book; preparing a food mentioned in the book; painting a scene from the book; writing a poem or readers theater script and performing it for an audience of teachers and students; designing a tableau; or engaging in some other creative activity that encourages self-expression and a meaningful response to the text.

After the club has finished a book, start another club for another grade level. If you finish a book in three weeks, you can have 12 book clubs over the course of a year. If ten students are in each club, you'll have had a significant impact on the literacy development of 120 students in one year! You'll have challenged them to participate in adult-type reading, and you'll be nurturing in them a habit that, hopefully, they'll carry into their adult lives.

We recall this line from the movie *Field of Dreams*: "If you build it, they will come." In regard to the Principal's Reading Club, the line might be, "If you start it, students will come, and other clubs will follow." It's one thing to have a Principal's Reading Club that immerses students more deeply in the reading experience, but let's face it: you can only work with so many students at a time. The ultimate aim is for your reading club to catch on and become very popular with students so others will replicate it. Encourage your faculty (and other members of your staff) to begin book clubs. Your faculty might choose books for their clubs that match their own interests. Thus, a wide range of genres could be covered with several book clubs in operation at one time. If each member of the faculty held one book club per semester, imagine the number of students your school could serve!

And if such clubs work well with faculty, there's no reason why you couldn't ask parents to sponsor book clubs in school and at home during the school year and during vacation. We know one parent who wanted to get her son more interested in reading, so she began a book club for him and five of his friends. She met with the six boys once a week. As a group, they chose the books to read and decided how much to read each week. They allowed their discussions to cover a wide range of ideas and issues raised in the books. Although the boys began meeting at the parent's home, they eventually arranged to meet in local restaurants, the community library, and a neighborhood bookstore. The boys loved their summer book club and read five books during the summer.

There's no telling where an idea like a Principal's Reading Club can lead. The best way to inspire reading among our best readers and among those students who struggle is to treat them the same way we would want to be treated when we read: We want a choice of interesting reading materials, comfortable surroundings, and opportunities to explore what we read in our own ways.

Summary

All students are different when it comes to reading. They differ in their levels of achievement, backgrounds, interests, and inspiration. As the instructional leader for your school, you need to ensure that policies and procedures exist to identify these differences and to do something about them when they affect students' learning. To the extent that individual differences hinder students' learning, you and your faculty need to work to help students overcome those hindrances. However, when individual differences add to the quality and diversity of your student population, you and your faculty should capitalize on those differences in order to inspire greater learning and deeper appreciation of what makes us all different.

Chapter 5: How Can Your Team Support Different Kinds of Learners?

117

CHAPTER 6

What Should You Know About Literacy Programs?

rs. Hemeseth is meeting with her second reading group at
the reading table for 30 minutes. After reviewing the assignment from the previous day, she engages her students in a lesson
on decoding multisyllabic words and makes a follow-up assignment to reinforce this critical skill. A brief topical and vocabulary
introduction to and discussion of the day's reading passage follows.
Then Mrs. Hemeseth sends her students to their individual tables
to begin their assigned work and calls the third group to meet
with her.

We had a chance to talk with Mrs. H. about her reading program. Here's what she had to say about it:

> We've had this reading program for the past four years, and I think it's terrific. In fact, most teachers like it. We had thought about developing our own program; we have a lot of experienced teachers on our faculty, but decided that it would work best for us teachers and our students if we relied on the collective wisdom of the reading field, and so we purchased the program we have now. We found that this program provides a strong emphasis on the essentials of reading—phonemic awareness, word decoding, reading fluency, vocabulary, and comprehension. I like it because it gives me just the amount of guidance I need to teach the essentials of reading, but at the same time I have the freedom to do some of the creative things that I have developed through the years with my kids.
>
> The last few years, we have seen a flock of new teachers come into our school. The baby boomer teachers are beginning to retire, and so the need [for the program] is there. These novice teachers love the program. Although they are new to the profession, we can be assured that, by following our instructional program, they are providing their students with instruction that is effective. There is no drop-off in quality in instruction because of a new teacher. The program we have developed is our assurance to parents and the community that the instruction students receive is consistent and of state-of-the-art quality.

Aside from an excellent teaching staff, the literacy program used for teaching reading is perhaps the most important component of literacy instruction in your school. Selecting and supporting the appropriate program can mean the difference between literacy education that runs smoothly and effectively throughout all grade levels and a literacy education curriculum that is marked by insufficient student progress, poor staff morale, and little buy-in to the program.

We have seen both the positive and the negative experiences occur. When an appropriate program is chosen and teachers feel a sense of ownership in it, they're more likely to implement the program with dedication and conviction to make it work for their students. They're more likely to coordinate their instruction with other teachers and with parents so that the literacy program makes sense to them. Thus, reading and reading instruction is sensible and effective. However, when teachers don't believe in a program, they're less likely to engage themselves as fully or as enthusiastically in its implementation. Teachers, administrators, parents—and especially students—suffer.

What types of reading programs are available?

There are many types of reading programs for the elementary grades. For the purposes of our discussion, we'll divide them into two main categories, comprehensive and specialized programs. Comprehensive programs attempt to be complete programs for teaching reading. Ideally, a teacher using a comprehensive reading program should require no other instructional materials. A specialized program, as the name implies, focuses on a particular area of reading. A specialized program might center on a particular curriculum area such as phonics or comprehension; it might focus on particular students such as struggling readers; or it might be aimed at supplemental instruction such as a home-involvement program or a summer reading program. Specialized programs are often seen as ancillary to a comprehensive reading program.

COMPREHENSIVE READING PROGRAMS

A comprehensive program attempts to be all things to all teachers and all children in a school. That's a pretty tall order. The advantages of a comprehensive program are obvious. In an ideal situation, comprehensive programs provide reading instruction that is seamless across grade levels and across the various types of children within each grade level. Two main types of comprehensive programs exist: basal reading programs and literature-based reading programs.

Basal reading programs: A basal reading program is designed by a commercial publisher of curriculum materials for schools. The publishing company brings together an author team of noted scholars in reading who set design criteria for a particular program. The publisher then develops the program based on the criteria established by the author team. Users of such a program take assurance in the fact that the program they purchase and employ is based on state-of-the-art theory and knowledge related to reading and incorporates the very best teaching materials and methods available.

Literature-based reading programs: The second type of reading program is most often called a literature-based program. It's designed locally by the teachers and administrators within a school or school district. The term "literature-based" is derived from the fact that the developers (school staff) use authentic literature (i.e., real books and other reading materials) as the material that students read. Literature-based programs are based on the belief that, since teachers in the local area are most knowledgeable about their students and the circumstances in which their students live, they're best able to design a reading program and choose reading materials that meet their students' needs and interests. Moreover, teachers often see the materials in commercially developed programs as not being real—they're engineered and altered to meet design specifications of text difficulty and length. They prefer to employ authentic material that doesn't alter the literary quality and authenticity of students' reading experiences.

Is one type of program better than the other? Although we may have our own preferences, we have to say that the choice of program depends on the principal, the faculty, and the students. If teachers feel knowledge-able enough about the reading process and how best to teach it, and they know their students, then empowering and supporting them to develop and implement their own reading program is ideal. However, the investment of time and resources for the development process and ongoing support can be enormous. On the other hand, if teachers feel more comfortable relying on the expertise of others for an instructional program, then a commercial basal is most appropriate. Indeed, in the United States, a huge majority of schools choose a basal reading program for their core reading curriculum.

We should note that it's entirely possible, and perhaps desirable, for a school to have a commercial basal program as the foundation for its literacy curriculum and then to enhance and supplement it with ancillary programs developed by teachers.

What should you look for in a reading program?

Regardless of whether you choose to use a commercially developed basal program or work with your faculty to design a reading program, certain features must be present in an effective program. You can use these features as the design criteria for developing your own program or as criteria to evaluate commercial programs that you're considering for purchase and adoption for your school. Each critical feature is explained briefly below. (At the end of this section, we include a chart that you can use to record your evaluations of a particular program.)

THE EFFECTIVE TEACHING OF READING

Over the last century, we've learned a lot about the teaching of reading. As we mentioned earlier, the National Reading Panel (NRP) reviewed the scientific research related to reading instruction and identified five key components of effective reading instruction: phonemic awareness, phonics or word decoding, reading fluency, vocabulary, and comprehension. The Panel argued that, based on the scientific evidence, reading instruction that is effective and state-of-the-art must include direct, intensive, and systematic instruction in these areas. The Panel didn't specifically state how these components should be taught, only that they be taught directly and consistently to students. As mentioned in Chapter 2, these components form the basis of what we feel is effective curriculum and instruction in reading. Whatever reading program your school chooses or develops, you, as the instructional leader, must ensure that these components appear in an appropriate manner within the program itself.

MEETING STANDARDS

Most states and many local school districts have developed standards for reading instruction. Clearly, when developing or choosing a program for instruction, be sure that the program aligns to the standards.

SUPPORT FOR TEACHERS

Is the program you choose or develop easy for teachers to implement, regardless of their level of expertise in teaching reading? Reading programs should have a well-developed teacher's guide that gives a succinct overview of the program's philosophy and approach and guides teachers in its implementation. The guide also should provide a scope and sequence overview to the program. Scope and sequence refers to the specific objectives and skills that are covered within a program and the grade level sequence in which they are presented to students. The guide should be easy to understand and to follow. In addition, it should provide teachers with a wide, but not overwhelming, array of instructional suggestions, ideas, and resources to use with students.

TEXT CONSIDERATIONS

The heart of any instructional program in reading is the texts that students read. Be sure to examine the nature and quality of the texts that are part of your instructional program for the following elements:

1. **The texts should be authentic.** They should be real stories, essays, and poems, and not material that was designed specifically to teach a particular reading skill or that was altered to fit within a particular grade level designation.

2. **Texts should reflect variety in genre, theme, and culture.** Although we think of stories or narratives as the essential material for a reading program, a truly effective program provides students with a diverse array of material to read. Your program certainly should include stories, but it also should include various forms of informational texts, essays, poetry, and other texts that are found in real life. Additionally, the reading materials should reflect diversity in topic, theme, and culture so students can have exposure to as wide a world as possible in their reading experiences.

3. **The difficulty of material is also an important consideration.** Be sure the materials that students read at various grade levels reflect appropriate levels of difficulty. This can be done through a technical analysis of the linguistic difficulty of the texts. Difficulty also should be weighed by qualitative analyses of the nature of the texts themselves: *Does the reading material deal with topics appropriate for a particular grade level? Are the passages an appropriate length? Is there anything in the text that others might find objectionable?*

INSTRUCTION

Although there is no one way to teach reading effectively to all students, we think it's important to examine ways in which instruction is presented in the reading program. Specifically, we believe in an approach to instruction that can be characterized as a *gradual release of responsibility*. To our way of thinking, any instruction works best when it begins with the teacher modeling what he or she intends students to gain. The modeling is then followed by guided practice in which students have the opportunity to engage in the learning activity under the guidance and support of the teacher and others who are able to assist the learner. Finally, students practice the learned activity independently. The teacher assesses students' performance and makes decisions about further follow-up and instruction. This approach to instruction should be apparent from an examination of the instructional lessons embedded in the program.

BALANCE

As we mentioned above, to our knowledge there is no one best way to teach students to read. Thus, in an effective program, we look for a degree of balance in what is offered to teachers and students. A program should have balance in the types of texts students are asked to read and the difficulty of reading material presented to students and the opportunity for oral and silent reading (a bias toward oral reading in the primary grades that moves toward greater amounts of silent reading in the upper grades). There also should be a balance between the following: teacher-guided reading and independent reading chosen by students; actual reading and a focus on reading-related skills students need to master.

GROUPING

In the elementary grades, students are normally taught reading in small groups. We think that grouping is an important part of an instructional program, but an effective program will allow teachers the opportunity to group students in a variety of ways. Look for reading instruction that's most often practiced in groups but that's also presented individually, in pairs, and in whole classroom groupings from time to time. Grouping students is most often done by achievement level: Students who are close to one another in reading achievement are often grouped together. While this is certainly one way to group, students also benefit from working with others who don't necessarily share their level of reading achievement. Ideally, we'd like to see opportunities for students to be grouped heterogeneously by achievement for instructional purposes. Other forms for grouping should also be encouraged—certainly grouping by interest is a natural and effective alternative to traditional forms of grouping.

MEETING INDIVIDUAL NEEDS

As we've discussed previously, any classroom will have students with different needs. Some students may have difficulty learning; others may be gifted in one or more areas; and for some, English may not be their first language. An effective reading program will provide teachers with instructional activities, ideas, and resources for meeting the individual needs of their students in an ongoing and systematic manner.

ASSESSMENT AND PROGRESS MONITORING

A strong reading program will have a corresponding program for assessing students' growth in reading and monitoring their ongoing progress throughout the school year embedded in it. The assessments should be valid measures of reading and its various subcomponents (e.g., decoding, fluency, and vocabulary) and not require large amounts of time to administer. Moreover, the assessment program also should provide teachers with efficient ways to record, analyze, and report the assessment results.

COORDINATION AND ALIGNMENT ACROSS AND WITHIN GRADE LEVELS

Be sure to examine the nature of transitions from one grade level to another. Does one grade level lead logically into the next in terms of passages read and skills taught? Will students (and teachers and parents) be able to detect the ongoing developmental nature of reading as presented by the program? Is there a level of consistency and alignment within grade levels? Teachers usually teach reading through reading groups within a classroom. Will the appropriate and necessary skills be taught regardless of grouping? Are there opportunities for students, regardless of instructional group membership, to work together on reading activities and projects throughout the school year?

FLEXIBILITY FOR TEACHERS

One defining feature of a school-based reading program is that it provides a level of coordination and consistency between and across grade levels. Regardless of the teacher, all students at a particular grade level will receive instruction in the same key areas of reading. However, not all teachers teach alike. A good program, regardless of whether it's locally developed or purchased, will give teachers enough flexibility to teach to their own styles and strengths without compromising the integrity of the school program as a whole.

HOME INVOLVEMENT

Literacy educators increasingly recognize the importance of parental and home involvement. An effective reading program will have an ongoing and systematic program for involving parents integrally in the reading development of their children.

Considering the criteria for selecting a reading program is a complex task that demands focus and time. In an effort to make it easier to have discussions with your staff around the above considerations, we have included a form for you to use as a tool with your faculty during discussions about reading program efficacy.

EVALUATION OF READING PROGRAM

Program: _____ **Publisher:** _____

Year: _____ **Grade Level(s):** _____

CRITERIA	COMMENTS
Effective Teaching of Reading	
Meeting Standards	
Teacher Support	
Text Considerations	
Instruction	
Balance	
Grouping	
Meeting Individual Needs	
Assessment and Progress Monitoring	
Coordination/Alignment Across and Within	
Grade Levels	
Flexibility for Teachers	
Home Involvement	

What is the best way to implement and support a literacy program?

Once your school chooses or develops a program, the next step is implementing it. Again, there's no one way to implement a program. We think a gradual implementation may have the best results for teachers and students. Ideally, a new literacy program should be implemented initially at the lowest possible grade level–kindergarten or Grade 1. Then, in each succeeding year, introduce the program to the next grade level.

The advantage of such an implementation is continuity. If an entire school moves from one program to another, the change for students who are in one program the previous year and are switched to a new program the following year can be quite disruptive: The change in materials, organization, and instructional approach can be confusing. On the other hand, kindergarten students who begin with the reading program in their first year of school will benefit from the continuity of the program from one grade level to another. As the program implementation moves from one grade level to the next, teachers in the preceding grade level can provide support and assistance for their colleagues who are now new to the program.

Unfortunately, this gradual introduction may not be possible. In most schools, the switch is school-wide for all grade levels and all students. If this is what's mandated for your school, it's important to provide support for teachers in their initial forays into the new program. You can achieve this through a series of professional development sessions aimed at implementing the program. These sessions should be well-planned by the school-wide literacy committee and should include, at a minimum, the following topics:

* An overview of the program and its guiding philosophy

* An overview of the materials in the program

* Daily instructional structure of the program, teaching the core lesson

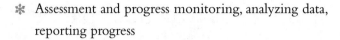

- ❋ Assessment and progress monitoring, analyzing data, reporting progress

- ❋ Meeting students' individual needs

- ❋ Coordination across and within grade levels

- ❋ Expanding and integrating a literacy program into other curricular areas.

Publishers often provide free professional development to schools in order to introduce their programs, and you should feel free to ask them to provide this service. However, be sure to take advantage of other areas of expertise in providing professional development for your staff. Presenters at sessions could include members of the literacy committee, teachers with experience with the program or one similar to it, teachers from other schools, university faculty, and other experts in your community. The more professional development you offer up front, the less likely you are to run into difficulties later on and the greater the likelihood that you will have full staff buy-in to the program and will enjoy the results you hope to achieve with it.

ANCILLARY PROGRAMS

An ongoing mission of your school literacy committee is to constantly evaluate the reading program in your school: *To what extent is it succeeding in producing optimal results? To what extent are the needs of all students being met?* The committee should regularly examine qualitative and quantitative data to assure itself that school-wide goals are being achieved. Unmet goals need to be addressed in some way.

One way to address unmet goals in literacy is through ancillary instructional reading programs. These are reading programs aimed at a particular component of reading (e.g., phonics and word decoding), a particular group of students (e.g., students learning English [ELL]), or a particular time and place for instruction (e.g., home involvement, summers). For example, if ongoing assessment and progress monitoring indicates that decoding is a concern for a large number of students and that, in general, students' achievement in decoding falls below expected norms, then an ancillary program in decoding to supplement the core reading program may be called for.

When areas of concern are noted and the use of an ancillary program is recommended, you need to work with your literacy committee and affected teachers to either purchase or develop an ancillary program for overcoming these areas. This will require the literacy committee to develop a set of design criteria, to examine various ancillary programs, and to choose (or develop) one that appears to be the best fit for your school.

Again, as with a core program, the selection or development of an ancillary program is just the beginning of your commitment to it. The implementation of such a program needs to be supported by professional development, the support of teachers, and the constant evaluation of how the program is working with your students and teachers.

SCHOOL AND CLASSROOM LIBRARIES

Books are essential to any reading program. Beyond the reading material in the core reading program and in other textbooks, students need access to a wide variety of reading material. The most appropriate repository for this material is the school library. Studies have shown that improvements in student reading achievement often come when schools significantly increase the amount of reading material available to students (book floods). The term *book flood* comes from the 1996 World Conference on Literacy in which schools in Fiji and Singapore who were teaching English as a second language, utilized the practice of "flooding" classrooms with books written in English as an augmentation to the curriculum used for English language instruction. Flooding a class with books is a technique that helps students become better readers and connect literacy to their real world. A book flood can be used in multiple contexts and generally refers to the practice of using significant amounts of quality literature to support the curriculum of a classroom.

Any school reading program worth its salt must have a large and varied library collection. As principal, you need to make extraordinary efforts to support your school's library. As with other important curricular decisions related to reading, we recommend that the school literacy committee take leadership in supporting the school library. However, recognizing your strong support for the school library will help the literacy committee make the library a priority.

Having a knowledgeable staff in the library/media center is key to the library's success. Your library staff must know books, how to get them into the hands of students, how to match students to books and other reading materials, and how to convince students that the books and materials in the library are worthy of their time and best efforts.

Financial and other support for the library is also essential. A librarian/media specialist who is savvy at supporting the library with grant money and fund-raisers is worth his or her weight in gold! However, this job shouldn't be left solely to the librarian. A library committee composed of parents, teachers, and the principal should take the responsibility of securing additional financial and volunteer support.

As principal, you set the example for the rest of the school. Become familiar with the school library. Make certain that students see you in the library browsing, selecting, and reading books; talking with students about favorite reads and learning about those books; and reading aloud to them. Use resources such as *Children's Choices* and *Teachers' Choices* to learn about books that you can read and recommend to students. As their names imply, these are annual selections of favorite children's books—one by children from across the country and the other by teachers. The results of previous years' competitions can be found at the Web site for the International Reading Association (IRA): www.reading.org. Both lists are great (and easy) ways to learn about books that kids and teachers would want to have in the school library.

SCHOOL BOOKROOM

A school bookroom is an essential part of your school's reading program. The bookroom is a repository of multiple copies of sets of books and other reading materials that teachers can check out and use. You need to make sure that your school has a bookroom and that you support it.

Even if a basal program is used as the core reading program in your school, there will be times when teachers will want to work with a group of students on a common book or article. Since it's expensive for a teacher to purchase multiple copies of a book to use for only a few weeks a year, and since more than one teacher may want to use the same title, it makes sense for the school to keep those books stored in a school bookroom. Teachers can check out the books and return them so other teachers may then borrow them for use in their classes.

As the materials in the school bookroom can only be accessed by teachers and other professional staff in your school, it can also act as the professional library for your staff. Keep current professional books and journals in the bookroom so they're available for teachers to read individually or in study groups.

Most schools in the United States don't have bookrooms of the type described above. However, we think it's essential for you to install one in your school and to support it through school resources. The more reading material we can get into students' hands, the more likely they're going to read and make progress in their development as readers.

CLASSROOM LIBRARIES

If reading material is important for reading achievement, well-stocked and well-supported classroom libraries are just as important as the school library and need to be considered as part of the overall school reading program. Although developing and maintaining a classroom library is largely the responsibility of the individual classroom teacher, you need to be aware that this is an important element of the reading program and should support it in any way you can. Encourage teachers to develop, maintain, and expand their classroom libraries. Provide moral and financial support for classroom libraries whenever possible. Perhaps a portion of each teacher's discretionary budget can be specifically directed to support his or her classroom library. Initiate school-wide book drives to build your school and classroom libraries. You also can call on the school literacy committee to assist teachers in their work in this area.

How can you set up special programs in your school?

When we first conceptualized this book, we felt that a chapter should be devoted to special reading programs for your school. Programs for struggling readers, gifted readers, and summer reading, we felt, deserved their own chapters. However, after some consideration, we decided to include these programs in the chapter that dealt with the overall school reading program. Although these programs may be aimed at particular groups of students, they need to be viewed in light of the entire school program. Although they are separate entities, they are also part of the whole.

LITERACY PROGRAM FOR STRUGGLING READERS

All schools have students who struggle in learning to read. Programs to support these students may include special education programs, federally funded Title I programs, or other programs aimed at giving a boost to students who are behind their classmates in their literacy development. Aspects of these programs are often dictated by the politics and policies of federal, state, and local governments, as well as by the school district itself. Other programs are dictated by the economic well-being of the students who attend your school. Thus, in many ways, you are limited in what you can do to establish such programs.

Regardless of the policy, principle, or rule that governs the program for struggling readers, we have some strong ideas about how programs for struggling readers are implemented in schools.

First and foremost, the program for struggling readers needs to maximize reading instruction for them. These students need all the instruction they can get in reading. Poor reading skills can lead to poor performance in other areas of the curriculum, so making sure students get as much reading instruction as possible is critical to their development. This may mean providing instructional periods that are significantly longer than what is provided to the normal school population. It may mean developing a program that is supplemental to the core reading program so students receive instruction that goes beyond their classroom reading program. Work diligently to ensure that your struggling readers receive their core instruction from the school's main literacy program as well as additional instruction from the special reading program. Support your teachers in ensuring coordinated instruction, so the various sources of instruction that students receive complement one another. In addition to longer periods for instruction, the instructional groups for struggling readers should be smaller than normal (e.g., groups of one to four students) so students can get additional and focused attention from their teacher.

The instructional program chosen for struggling readers can be developed locally or it can be purchased through commercial channels. Regardless of the source, it's important to note that the needs of struggling readers are largely the same as for all readers. That is, instructional programs for struggling readers should incorporate the same focal areas for instruction—phonemic awareness, phonics and decoding, fluency, vocabulary, and comprehension—and they should be judged using the criteria noted earlier in this chapter. What these students need is not something completely new but more intensive instruction that's focused on areas in which they demonstrate marked deficiency. Programs that diverge from these focal areas or that ask students to engage in activities that don't involve real reading should be avoided.

LITERACY PROGRAMS FOR GIFTED READERS

We think that all students are gifted in one way or another. With that in mind, all teachers should be expected to provide literacy experiences that challenge students' creativity and imagination.

Certainly, students whose reading achievement is well above their assigned grade level need reading material that challenges them. This is true of all readers, not just those who are exceptionally good readers. So the maxim of having a wide variety of material that covers a wide range of difficulty levels applies here. The school literacy committee and the library committee need to ensure that such material is available to teachers and students and that everyone is aware of its existence.

We think that all teachers should bear the responsibility, or the privilege, of providing all students with literacy learning activities that expand their horizons. Moreover, we believe that such activities cannot easily be put into a boxed commercial program. Rather, they need to originate from the interests of students and teachers as well as from the culture of the school and community in which it is located.

One more point: To be considered literacy activities, these activities need to have reading and writing at their core. Simply reading a book or poem and then creating a piece of artwork in response to it is only partially a literacy experience. We would like to see the response activity include literacy in use. Below, we present some examples of literacy activities that tap into the gifted and creative nature of all students.

EXAMPLES OF LITERACY ACTIVITIES FOR THE GIFTED AND CREATIVE NATURE OF ALL STUDENTS

- Students write poetry in response to a book they have read or an experience they have had. The poetry is performed at a classroom poetry slam and is later typed, duplicated, bound, and published.

- During Women's History Month, students work in small groups to write short readers-theater scripts based on stories of famous women they have read about and researched.

- Students do an oral history of a family member and then write it up as a biography. The individual biographies are collected and published as a class book.

- Students run a biweekly school newspaper that features school-based articles and stories as well as other elements that are found in a typical newspaper (e.g., letters to the editor, advice column, comics).

- Students write, perform, and publish parodies to familiar songs and poems.

- During African-American History Month, students study famous oratory from the civil rights era and then write and perform speeches that reflect and honor the African-American experience.

How do you support your teachers in developing and employing the creative touch in their literacy education curriculum? There is no easy answer to this question. As we said earlier, the answer is not in some pre-packaged program for teachers of the gifted. We think the answer lies with teachers themselves. We need to give them opportunities to share with one another some of the exciting projects they've developed for their students. Regular staff meetings can be devoted to sharing creative literacy projects with opportunities for other teachers to consider how they might adapt the project for their own students and circumstances. Shared projects also can be archived on a teacher resource Web site.

LITERACY PROGRAMS FOR LINGUISTICALLY DIVERSE STUDENTS

Historically, the United States has been a linguistically and culturally diverse nation. The immigrant experience in this country has given schools the responsibility of teaching English to students. To this day, schools around the country enroll students whose ability to communicate in English is limited.

If your school has students whose English skills are limited, you must ensure that these students are provided support in learning English. Again, there is no one best way to teach reading. This certainly applies to teaching English Language Learners (ELL students). There are various schools of thought regarding how best to teach these students basic English skills— through immersion in English or through a transitional program in which they make gradual connections between their first language and English.

The decision on which approach to take is one that we feel should be made at the school or school district level. Regardless of the approach, if you have ELL students in your school, it's critical that you make ELL literacy instruction a priority. You must ensure that you and your school literacy committee monitor the ELL literacy program and support teachers in their work with ELL students.

Language diversity is a reflection of the cultural diversity inherent among students. Please be sure to make a priority of honoring and celebrating the cultural heritage of all students throughout the year. Not only will this make ELL students and families feel more welcome in the school community, it will help nurture the sense of respect and tolerance for everyone that is a critical goal for schools.

Summary

Literacy instruction is often defined by the literacy program that a school develops or adopts. As we've discussed in this chapter, there are many dimensions to a school's literacy program. Although we don't feel it's the principal's duty to mandate a particular program or programs to be employed in a school, it is the principal's duty to take a leadership role in selecting and then supporting the programs that are chosen or developed. In selecting and supporting a literacy program, the principal must keep teachers' and students' eyes on the prize of full literacy for all students. This is done by guiding teachers in making informed decisions about the program they choose, supporting and empowering them to make the program most effective for students, and monitoring the program to ensure fidelity in its application for all students. These are tough tasks, no doubt, but they are some of the most important tasks a principal can undertake in ensuring literacy for all students.

CHAPTER 7

Why Is Leadership So Important in Implementing and Supporting Literacy Programs?

Nick Phillips is an elementary school principal in a small town that's an hour's drive outside of Pittsburgh, Pennsylvania. He serves a school that has achieved modest standardized test score results. Nick is well loved by his faculty, staff, and community. Moreover, he's enjoyed every one of the six years he's served as the instructional leader at John Dewey Elementary School. Nick is particularly proud of the fact that he never let go of his roots as a fourth-grade teacher. He still reads professional journals and regularly covers classes as a substitute teacher for his staff.

When we spoke with Nick, he had just come back from a week-long staff development conference that his school district administrator had asked him to attend. He shared the following with us:

I always feel uncomfortable when I go to these conferences because I can't stand being away from my building. It is so hard to get away, even in the summer. There is so much I need to do at school. But usually by the second day of the conference I get interested in the presentations and the possibilities for our school. This year, my school leadership team came with me to a workshop in Pittsburgh. Like all the other years at these things, we talked during the drive home from the conference about what we could do with the new ideas presented. This time though, I felt a little jaded. I'm not jaded about the kids or the staff, or even the community. I am just frustrated because I have been around long enough to see the way things work.

You see, it seems like every summer our staff leadership team is directed to go to a retreat, institute, or "thing" that the curriculum guys have deemed important. Mind you, our curriculum staff is wonderful at the district office, but none of them has ever been an administrator at a school. Not one of the people who select the staff development program has been a principal. We have one curriculum director who used to be the athletic director for the district and the other director used to teach special education, but no former principals. I think their background makes a difference in how decisions in our district are made. There is a gap sometimes between what the district wants us to do and what we need to do. It has gotten to the point where I can now bank on the fact that I will be required to attend a day-long principals' meeting in September when I am trying to ease my school into a new school year. This is very frustrating. And then at this meeting I will be in-serviced on all the things we need to do to create a plan and implement the ideas we saw at the retreat 12 weeks before. So I scramble, my staff scrambles, and we make some sort of plan within the framework of the stuff we heard at the retreat to show the public at a governing board meeting.

In the midst of all the scrambling, questions come up about how this new plan will really play out in our classrooms. The standard answer we get from the consultants or district curriculum facilitators is, "Don't worry about that part right now" or "We have a team of people working on that and we will let you know."

Here is the problem: They never do let us know. Because the truth is, they don't know. So we are faced with implementing a plan that looks good at first glance but fails in lots of places when scrutinized. It seems like our school district is always part of some grant run by someone who fails to have a realistic understanding of curriculum or has no clue about how schools operate, and so they have no real answers for the questions we ask. The superintendent is concerned about just making sure stuff is going smoothly, and the grant directors are about making sure that the superintendent only hears that everything is smooth.

Half the time, I think the grant writers are surprised when our district actually gets the grant that they submitted an application for. The response I hear most of the time is, "Don't worry; these ideas are based on best practices." Best practice according to whom? You know, I am never worried. What I am is skeptical. It seems to me that a lot of folks throw the phrase "best practice" around as if it were this thing that validates whatever new idea we need to hurry up and embrace so that our school or district can validate its existence.

I love our school and am still energized about my job. And I love trying to make things better in the classroom for our teachers and students. I just have no desire to lose my credibility trying to sell "best practice" this and "best practice" that to a group of teachers I admire and respect.

Nick's story is typical of the frustrations we've found among principals trying to find their way as leaders in the choppy seas of professional development and school reform. School administration is particularly difficult in terms of curriculum reform because, as a frontline administrator, the principal must negotiate the realities between the vision of the grant sponsors; the demands of the district officials trying to accommodate the sponsors; and the reality of limited resources in terms of staff, supplies, and time. This chapter is dedicated to looking at this sticky leadership challenge by focusing on leadership issues as they relate to the selection and implementation of literacy programs.

How should you approach a literacy program that "everyone" loves?

The hard part about attending a conference is first learning to detach ourselves from all the details swirling around in our building but, like Nick, once we do, we usually get excited about what we're talking about with our colleagues in a national forum.

Being at a professional development conference is sort of like being at a pep rally. The presenters are typically thrilled to proselytize the good news about all the effective and efficient things they've been doing at the schools in their community; however, conference attendees often choose a specific session because it was recommended or mandated by the higher ups in their school district.

After the presentation, members of the captive audience approach the speaker with specific questions or a request for a business card. This can (and often does) lead to a chain of events that starts the collaboration process between a school district and a speaker, who is now deemed a consultant. The attendees leave, enthusiastically looking forward to working with a consultant who will have some answers for the problems at their school. Then, just like in Nick's story, they get back to the reality of their school's culture, and the problems are stickier than they seemed in the heady intellectual haze of the conference.

Before you go to your next conference, we suggest you make a small investment that will lower the sense of frustration that can occur after the professional pep rally ends: Prepare yourself to recognize a phenomenon called "The Abilene Paradox" (Harvey, 1988). Essentially, the Abilene Paradox is an allegory about a group of people living in Texas who decide to drive a long distance through the hot desert in order eat dinner at a cafeteria in Abilene, a town many uncomfortable miles away. After a tiresome journey and a mediocre dinner, one of the people finally admits that they didn't want to go to Abilene at all—they went simply to be gracious. This revelation leads to all members of the group ultimately confessing that they, too, went only to please the other members of the group. In essence, the group took an action that contradicted what its members really wanted to do.

What does driving through a Texas desert have to do with leadership? Harvey argues that this illogic also can be found within the politics of organizations. We argue (as would most educators) that school systems are not only organizations, they are extremely complex organizations. The corollary of the Abilene Paradox states that organizations frequently take actions in contradiction to the data they have for dealing with problems and, as a result, they compound their problems rather than solving them. Like many paradoxes, the Abilene Paradox deals with absurdity. At first glance, it makes little sense that school systems take such absurd actions; however, we've outlined and explained the reasons for the Abilene Paradox. As you read through Harvey's frameworks, consider how (or if) they're congruent with your own experiences in your school district.

ACTION ANXIETY

Action anxiety is based on the premise that members of an organization take action in direct contradiction to their understanding of the organization's problems. They do this because they believe that contradicting the boss will get them into trouble. As a result of this anxiety, the decision-makers opt to pursue an unworkable research project or participate in a feckless reform endeavor rather than acting in a way that aligns with their beliefs. In other words, administrators or other leaders find themselves wrestling with the following question:

> Is it better to maintain my sense of integrity and make the
> boss mad at me, or should I just agree with the reform plan
> or project so that the boss doesn't give me any hell?

NEGATIVE FANTASIES

Harvey explains that part of why Action Anxiety occurs is due to the negative fantasies members of an organization have about what will happen if they act in accordance with their understanding of what is sensible. For example, a school principal may think the following:

> If I tell the new curriculum coordinator, who is best friends
> with the superintendent, that this grant is not going to raise
> test scores because it's geared for smaller rural schools
> and our school is large and in the inner city, I know he'll go
> straight to the superintendent and tell her that I'm not a
> team player. Then the superintendent will get mad at me for
> not being a team player, and she could move me to a district
> office administrative job, or she could move me to another
> school. I do not want that. I only have two years to go until
> retirement so there's no sense in making waves now.

Fantasies like this provide the individual with an excuse that releases him or her psychologically from the responsibility of having to act to solve the problems within an organization.

REAL RISK

Harvey (1988) argues that within the fantasies described above the amount of risk is an existential condition. In other words, the principal who's worried about getting fired or moved needs to ask him or herself, *Will I really get fired? Will my life really be more difficult?* In reality, no, the principal probably won't be fired, but we do fear things that we have either experienced or have witnessed others experience. The most common type of fear is separation and professional alienation. If you have trouble buying into the idea that the fear of disconnectedness can drive us to avoid real risk, consider what our society believes to be one of the ultimate punishments for prisoners serving a life sentence: solitary confinement.

The fear of taking a risk that results in our own professional ostracism is at the core of the Abilene Paradox. As leaders, we may rationalize this fear (and justly so) as a way of playing politics to preserve our own careers or to preserve what we perceive to be the righteous path of our school. Unfortunately, the unspoken fear of separation can result in research committees, curriculum committees, and/or school governing boards supporting actions that many, some, or none of its members really want.

How do you avoid the Abilene Paradox?

From a systemic point of view, the first step in avoiding this paradox is to avoid blaming other people when things go wrong. When a system is mired in finger pointing, energy is drained away from legitimate and productive problem solving. Secondly, it's important to note the importance of real conflict and phony conflict. Real conflict is when people in a system have real differences about situations, decisions, and so on. Phony conflict is when members of a group agree on a particular course of action, and do the opposite. For example, if a group of principals agrees with the curriculum director that they will all adopt a block schedule, and then one principal fails to do so, the result is a sense of frustration and mistrust on the part of his or her colleagues. Furthermore, if the rogue principal is not held accountable for his refusal to follow through with the agreement he made, then the principal's colleagues become frustrated not only with the rebellious leader but also with the superintendent and other superiors who allowed the behavior to go on without consequences. This can have a domino effect in a school district where, over time, many people choose not to "buy into" the vision.

CONFRONTING THE PARADOX

You can go along the road to Abilene and reflect on why you're doing it, or you can attempt to explain to your colleagues what you think is happening within the culture of your workplace. Harvey (1988) calls this "confronting." If you choose to confront, it's important to do so within a group setting, since the Paradox results from dysfunctional group dynamics. For example, suppose you believe that the restructuring effort your entire school district is undertaking as a result of a million-dollar grant is on the road to Abilene. Specifically, you've decided that a three-month timeline to implement a new literacy instruction model without the support of a strong teacher evaluation instrument and in-depth staff training is not healthy for your school district or its students.

The first thing you need to do is be prepared to share your objections with the group most responsible for the decisions in an arena that's appropriate. A governing board meeting is not an appropriate venue for your concerns, but a district-level administrators' meeting might be. When you share your concerns about an issue, you need to make sure your comments are offered in a non-threatening tone of voice.

We've contoured Harvey's (1988) suggested comments to fit within the culture of a school system. Read the following to see how you might approach confronting the Abilene Paradox:

> I've been thinking about our reform plan. While I'm thrilled we have the financial support of our grant, I believe that I've said some things about the plan that are contrary to what I think about its viability. I also don't believe I'm the only person who

feels this way about certain parts of this plan. Specifically, I'm concerned about the realistic way of implementing this district-wide grant when it doesn't allow for a summer bridge program. There is a recognizable literacy gap between elementary school and high school, and I know from conversations with my colleagues that many of us are in agreement about the value of a summer bridge program. When we're told that this idea doesn't fit into the grant, I wonder if we're forgetting that our primary goal is to look for ways to help students, rather than to look for ways to fit the exact requirements of a grant. I'd like for our group to consider having a frank discussion about what we believe about the summer bridge program and its relevance to our schools.

When (or if) you decide to confront, there will be one of two outcomes depending on the leadership of its members.

A. The group will decide to consider the concerns and, as a group, the organization will make strides to address the technical issues raised by your confrontation, and the Abilene Paradox will be broken, or

B. You will be thanked for your input, essentially ignored, and the Abilene Paradox will continue.

If outcome A happens, take pride in your courage, convictions, and leadership and know that you've contributed to ending the Abilene Paradox. If outcome B happens, take pride in your courage, convictions, and leadership and consider if you want to continue working in an organization that ignores the realities of problem solving. If outcome B happens, does that mean you need to find another job? For some people, it does. For others, the decision to leave happens after many futile confrontations over trips to Abilene. This life-defining moment is described best by Ellen, the principal of a 1,200-student inner city K–8 school we met at the National Association of Elementary Principals' 2004 annual convention in San Francisco, California.

I had been a principal for 11 years at the same K-8 inner city school in a large urban district. I enjoyed my staff, but the truth was that by year five I felt that my primary job was to make the road easier for the higher-ups by not making waves. All of this seemed to be at the expense of our kids. The expenses seemed little, like a refusal to deal with a lack of support staff funds, or the tail-spinning of a committee to decide on community resources. The problem for me was that the little things started to add up in my mind. In my third year as principal, I was told to back off of an instructional improvement plan I was implementing with a teacher because there was a fear that her husband, a member of the negotiations team, would use that information to make contract talks more difficult. And then I watched during my fifth year a heated disagreement between members of the governing board about the colors that were to be chosen for a new school. I could not believe that this was the important issue for them, yet they chose not to discuss the merits of funding an all-day kindergarten program. It seemed like no one wanted to deal with controversial issues that required folks to make a clear decision. Frankly, I understood that this particular year was a contract rene-gotiation year for the superintendent, but I remember the last time something like this happened. It was the superintendent's first year in the position with a new board, so we let the more provocative issues stay in the background. And the year before that, I remember that there were no provocative decisions because the superintendent was in his last year before retire-ment and wanted to coast. It just seemed like there was always an excuse for our community to deal with paint chips and mascot choices rather than with a shortage of resources for school improvements or changing expectations on teaching instruments. I hold no malice toward that superintendent; he was simply trying to steer through the political waters.

I was respected in this district, mostly I think, because I kept my mouth shut. I no longer liked that feeling. I got tired of being told in administrative council meetings, "That's a good idea but the union won't go for that, and we really need to focus on this instead." I think I realized that maybe I had changed, the district culture had changed, or both. Basically, I just did not feel like I fit anymore.

Once I understood this, I knew it was time to go. I did not complain, I did not make waves, but I did start thinking about where I wanted to go and what I wanted to do. A year after I knew it was time to leave, I got a principalship at another school in a district that is a 45-minute drive father away from my home. I don't care. Even though I have to drive farther, I feel renewed at this school and excited about the challenges. I was so scared about moving because I thought I would retire in my old school district. When I left, some people could not understand why, especially since my own daughter had attended and graduated from my school. But leaving was the best thing that ever happened to me.

The decision to leave based on the futility of attempting to break the Abilene Paradox is often described by some administrators as "no longer fitting." Does this mean you're a bad leader? Absolutely not. In many cases, the process of realizing one doesn't fit, identifying why (which can happen through the act of confronting), and then making a choice to move on is an existential experience that results in a stronger sense of self. Often, these self-realized leaders are the people you meet, like our friend Ellen, who will say, "Leaving school district XYZ was the best thing that ever happened to me." Ultimately, the decision to leave or stay is a very personal one. What is important from our point of view is that you begin to recognize the symptoms of the Abilene Paradox as they pertain to how your school district embraces the next new "thing."

What should your response be when you hear "best practice" and "research based"?

Much like other widely used adjectives within the educators' lexicon, the concept of "best practice" implies a sort of academic or professional endorsement of the choices or plans we're implementing in our schools. In many cases "best practices" are gleaned from efforts grounded in pedagogical research. For example, this book is an example of "best practices" because it speaks to the research that we've found or generated in the academic community. That means that we had to adhere to some specific guidelines concerning the authenticity of our efforts. Many other books adhere to the same sorts of standards. You'll be able to recognize these efforts when the author(s) or other experts can, with some ease, explain the research that their "research-based" practice is based on. In some school systems, "best practice" enters discussions in the organizational culture without its partner "research-based." Another conundrum is that the adoption of a curriculum delivery model can be inconsistent within a school district because the team or person in charge of implementing "research-based practices" does not really have a grasp of the concept. This scenario makes us wonder the following: *How does one hold people accountable for implementing a program that one does not fully understand?* In this case, we find that a phrase such as "research-based model" evolves into an ambiguous description of what everyone is doing within a district, and yet the implementation is inconsistent. Here again, the road to Abilene beckons.

We found a great example of how "best practice" has mutated into a nonsensical phrase when we talked to Jim, one of our favorite principals, at a local middle school. When we asked him in a casual conversation about the literacy plan at his school, he replied, "We're doing Best Practices." We asked, "Best practice according to whom?" The question surprised Jim. He answered, "I don't know. When I go to the staff development, it's just 'best practice.' That's how our district describes our new reform model." So then we asked, "What does best practice mean at your school in terms of the fourth-grade classroom?" Jim replied, "Well, that's an interesting question because at my school in the fourth grade, we're including year-long themes in local history, but at my colleague's school, he's doing best practice by using drama as part of the instructional delivery. We wanted to highlight drama in the fourth grade too, but we couldn't as our district is following a niche marketing model. So our school is supposed to focus on the thematic strand and their school is using the dramatic integration strand. You would think we could do both, but the training for drama in literacy instruction was available for their magnet school only, so our teachers couldn't go. Our teachers instead went to the interactive history training."

After a little more probing what we learned was that "best practice" in this district's culture refers to a pastiche of techniques and teaching ideas from different models. However, when we talked to seven other principals in this same district, none was able to articulate an understanding of their district's approach to literacy instruction further than the statement of "best practice." Furthermore, everyone's definition of the phrase differed. This led us to conclude that if everyone's idea of best practice is different, then in reality there's no standard that the phrase "best practice" would imply.

Does this sound familiar to you? If so, make a point to learn about literacy so that you can confidently ask the technical questions that help to prevent the Abilene Paradox from happening in your district. Refer again to Chapter 2 when you're introduced to a new literacy model or program and use the basic knowledge presented there to help you form a conceptual understanding of how the new program stacks up against the research on quality literacy instruction. When you see gaps between the new program being considered and what you know about literacy, don't be afraid to mention them.

Understand that there is a difference between program delivery models and teaching techniques. A program delivery model incorporates various teaching techniques and addresses issues of contouring the culture of a school (and district) to honor the tenets of a program. Teaching techniques are those specific instructional tips that can be used in a classroom to help support the overall vision of a model. Teachers are often given the teaching tips without a proper focus on the larger context of the delivery model. This is an important mistake because when teachers are excluded from the overall understanding of what they are doing, they can fail in terms of actually implementing the literacy program that a school or school district has adopted.

What should you do when a workshop feels like a waste of time?

Sometimes, even the best intentions of workshop sponsors go awry, and sometimes, a negative experience is rooted in the experience of the participant. This is what Susan, a principal in her second year, had to say about her participation in a workshop on building literacy in San Diego.

> I hated it. I was tired. I did not want to sing with everyone else. So basically I felt a little uncomfortable to begin with. Then this facilitator guy broke us into small groups of six people. I knew no one in my group, but I was fine with that. Our facilitator, Pablo, gave us a piece of paper in the shape of a bridge. He said this was a great example of how to get students warmed up for writing and self-reflection. So then he asked us to write on the "bridge" examples of three times in our lives when we had to really struggle to cross a bridge over pain or tragedy. I just froze. I know that in workshops a lot of times we all are supposed to bond, but I am a very private person and I was there in a very public arena with people I did not know. I was not about to talk about the tragedies in my life. And frankly I felt very uncomfortable when Pablo then asked us to talk about what we wrote. Then Pablo gave me some grief because I did not really write on my bridge. I just shut down. And I turned off the rest of the conference because of that sharing exercise. It may seem extreme but being tired and doing things that pushed me a little out of

my shell only made me feel more vulnerable. I still did not understand the point of the exercise. I came here to learn about a
whole program model—not engage in therapy. Furthermore, I still
don't understand what this exercise had to do with the delivery
model we were supposed to be learning about. I feel like I don't
have the entire picture.

The lesson for Susan, and for you, is that if you have a less than positive experience at one point in a retreat or a workshop, don't let it fog your ability to be open to learning other new things. Give yourself a break in a situation like this. Skip a session in order to clear your head or revital-ize yourself. Usually conferences are geared so that participants can take advantage of down time. If your mind and spirits are rested, then you're better able to concentrate on what a facilitator is asking you to do. You're also better able to articulate why you feel uncomfortable with an activity. A skilled facilitator should be able to utilize your insights as a way to brain-storm as a group about the challenges that teachers face in the classroom. Shutting down doesn't allow you the chance to learn, and it cheats the facilitator out of valuable feedback so he or she can reconsider how to deliver the message.

When you feel as though you've had less than a quality training experi-ence, give yourself a mental break from the group. Then reflect on why the experience wasn't as good as it could have been for you. Was the facilitator's style incongruent with yours? Perhaps you weren't as prepared for the workshop as you would have liked to have been in terms of reading the suggested materials. Were you tired because you didn't get as much sleep as you needed? Maybe it was difficult to ask questions because the facilitator wasn't engaging or appeared to be unprepared. Remember your experi-ences when you're conducting staff development at your own school; be considerate of your participants.

Finally, honor the importance of a little detective work. When you're introduced to a new model or idea, learn about the authors through their other works. Most curriculum experts share their work histories on the Internet. You can either enter their names at www.google.com or www.scholar.google.com to learn about their accomplishments and areas of expertise.

If the author or expert you're learning about is a professor, make sure you visit the Web site of the university at which he or she is employed. Find out if this expert is affiliated with a reputable literacy consortia or has done comparable work in schools similar to your own. The International Reading Association (IRA) is the premier professional organization in this country for teachers, professors, and experts in the field of literacy. Their Web site, www.reading.org, has a myriad of resources that will help you to learn more about the literacy professionals your school district is working with and the innovations they're encouraging you to adopt. Also, ask yourself if these ideas have been discussed in the IRA publication, *The Reading Teacher*.

Another very powerful question you can ask concerning a new idea is if it's research-based. If it is, then the next question a savvy principal asks is the following: *Whose research is this program based on, and where can I find this research?* When you're told that something is "data driven," don't be afraid to ask whose data and where you can find the data. Again, the respondent to your questions should be able, with relative ease, to direct you to a reputable source (like the ones mentioned above) to examine the data. The efforts you make to ask these questions will help you better understand how the literacy program you're considering is grounded and accepted in other academic arenas and school systems.

Why is it so important
to attend staff trainings?

It's arguably more important for you, the administrator, to attend the teacher in-services than for your staff, because you have to be able to understand what your teachers are supposed to be doing. The reality of the district staff development day is that usually teachers are assigned to various workshops and administrators are asked to attend meetings or to be at the school site to answer questions. As a principal, you may feel relieved because this time will allow you to catch up on paperwork. *Don't cheat yourself.* When there's a district staff development day (and you aren't responsible for doing the development), choose the area that you feel weakest about in terms of instruction and attend the training with the teachers. You'll earn credibility with your staff, and you'll gain a clearer understanding of just what you should be looking for in a classroom evaluation. Your consistent presence at staff development clearly demonstrates to your staff that you're serious about instruction as a learner and as an evaluator. It also allows you to see what your teachers are experiencing.

If you find yourself in a district that schedules staff development in such a way that principals are not able to participate in the workshops for teachers, ask those in charge if it's possible to change that practice. Explain why it's a good idea to share the training experience with your staff. Asking can't hurt. The worst thing that can happen is you get another chance to see if you and your colleagues are on the road to Abilene.

What do you need to do when you bring in a speaker for staff development?

It's always exciting to bring in a speaker you've heard or read about to your school. If you have the opportunity, take full advantage of it by doing some homework. Ask yourself the following list of questions when you're negotiating a visit with a speaker:

QUESTIONS ABOUT THE SPEAKER

* What is it that I liked about the speaker's style, book, and so on? How did that show me that he or she would be a good fit for our school?

* What if this speaker is someone that I really want to invite to my school, but I don't have the funds? Does he or she have an "apostle" who can visit our school for a lower fee instead?

* What does the speaker need me to do to prepare my staff for his or her visit?

* Is the speaker willing to stay after the teacher in-service and meet again with parents, community members, or our shared leadership development team?

* What can I do to make the speaker's stay as comfortable as possible in terms of technology, supplies, refreshments, lodging, and "down time"?

* Are there any data the speaker would like me to gather (surveys and so on) before his or her visit?

- What do I need to explain to the speaker about payment (e.g., when the district office will generate payment, and how payment will be delivered)?

- Is the speaker willing to discuss follow-up visits or a package of collaboration with my staff?

- Do I know anyone who has worked with this speaker? What was that experience like?

- What do I want the speaker to focus on during his or her presentation?

- If the speaker is entering into a collaboration with us, is he or she willing to write or present a brief report of our efforts to our district's Board of Education?

QUESTIONS ABOUT THE MEETING

- What are some examples I can show the speaker of his or her ideas in action?

- What are some examples of glitches I can show that need his or her input?

- Before the speaker arrives, what does he or she need to know about our staff in terms of their strengths, weaknesses, and focus for this academic year?

- Can the visit be structured so that I can give the speaker a tour around the building and allow him or her to get a flavor for the school culture before he or she engages our staff?

- Can I schedule the speaker's visit so that I can also attend it and participate?

QUESTIONS ABOUT THE STAFF

✳ Do I need to remind my staff how to act at an in-service toward a guest? Does my staff understand that my minimum expectation is that they pay attention and are polite?

✳ How will I hold my staff accountable for participating in this in-service and implementing the ideas presented?

✳ Which of our staff's goals for the year are specifically related to this speaker?

✳ How can I ensure that my staff will have read this speaker's book or article before our in-service together?

✳ Is there anyone at the district office that I should invite to this speaker's in-service?

Investing in professional development is one of the most challenging responsibilities of the principalship because it is so easy to avoid the process of thinking ahead. Also, it is difficult to point out weakness in a program to colleagues and superiors once a program has been selected. The challenge of supporting teachers demands a vigilant focus on program implementation and accountability. These daily demands can be trumped easily by more dramatic challenges such as classroom discipline issues, micro-politics, and community needs. Don't let these daily fires steal time away from a focus on your school's future; doing so will only lead to last minute planning for professional development activities. Sadly, this often results in the implementation of support for teachers that has limited credibility in the classroom and low impact on student learning.

What are some ideas for literacy-centered staff development that you can use each month?

What do you do if you're trying to find solid, concrete staff development activities to help your staff focus on literacy? The best way to approach this question, from our view, is to apply a mindset similar to the teacher who's planning the year in the classroom. Simply get a calendar and brainstorm one "literacy staff event" for your teachers and support staff. These professional development opportunities don't have to be built on consultants and guest speakers.

We offer the following calendar of ideas below as a springboard for your staff development plan:

AUGUST: *Welcome Back to School In-service*

Main questions for staff meeting:

* What is reading? How do children read?

* What are the three big views on how one learns to read (top-down, bottom-up, and interactive processing)?

* What key factors affect children's ability to read?

Activity: Distribute a newspaper, Web page, or copies of a book page in another language to staff so they remember what it's like to struggle with word comprehension, text, and letter recognition. Russian or Greek are particularly useful for this project as some of the alphabet will be unfamiliar to most staff members. Poems from Shel Silverstein's *Runny Babbit* also provide examples of delightful texts that are challenging to read fluently and to comprehend. Begin the activity by inviting a staff member to read the text aloud. Next invite the staff to read a second piece in Spanish, French, or German (as some words will look familiar to them). Ask the staff to reflect on the experience and to discuss what it was like reading these pieces. Have them to compare their insights to what their students might be experiencing. Finally, use the information in Chapter 2 to explore with your staff how children learn to read and what affects their learning.

SEPTEMBER

Main question for staff meeting:

※ What is The National Reading Panel, and what did they say that was relevant to me? Use the information in Chapter 2 to discuss the formation of the National Reading Panel and its importance. Also review and discuss the five essential parts of reading as discussed by the Panel:

  1. phonemic awareness

  2. phonics

  3. fluency

  4. vocabulary

  5. comprehension

Activity: Before your staff in-service, ask teams from each grade level to prepare a presentation on one of the five essential parts to give to the rest of the staff. Invite the staff teams to create an activity for their colleagues that emphasizes their assigned topic. For example, the fourth-grade team who was charged with talking about vocabulary might change a common nursery rhyme into something more difficult to understand by switching the vocabulary around. This new rhyme could be a puzzle for the staff to figure out as an opening set to their presentation. For example, the 1830 poem "Mary Had a Little Lamb" by Sarah Joseph Hale could be presented to the staff in the following way:

> The young Maria possessed an ovis aries who was petite for its age. The follicles that protected the dermis of this mammal reflected all the colors in the light spectrum much like the crystals that form on the tops of Mont Blanc in the tenth month of the year. Wherever the young lady traveled, moreover, her quadruped was certainly in pursuit.

Then the vocabulary team might break the staff into groups and ask them to change a favorite familiar poem or quotation. After groups share their results, the teacher leading the discussion can talk about why a foundation in vocabulary is so important and give a few ideas for classroom activities (including changing the words of a poem) to build students' vocabulary.

OCTOBER

Main questions for staff meeting:

* Who are our struggling readers?

* How do we identify them?

* Which strategies are we using to help these students?

Activities: Utilize help from the district office curriculum division to help you interpret standardized test scores from the previous year. Are students in a particular grade struggling with reading? In what specific areas do the scores show a difficulty? Reread Chapter 5 to find a framework of ideas to present to your staff. Meet individually with each grade-level team, and bring along your reading specialist, to discuss the test scores and how the teachers have identified struggling readers in their classes. Ask your grade-level teams to prepare for this meeting so they'll be able to present concrete information on how they've identified struggling readers. After their presentations, engage the teams in discussions with your reading specialist about strategies each teacher will use to engage struggling readers and to support them.

You can also augment these individual team meetings with a staff meeting designed to let your teachers share other strategies they've had success with in the classroom. Set up the meeting with a series of round-table discussions. Invite your strongest teachers in each grade to give 15-minute presentations (with handouts) to their colleagues. Ring a bell or blow a whistle so that every 15 minutes teachers are moving from one round-table presentation to the next. After everyone has attended all the presentations, bring the entire staff back into a large group to discuss what they learned.

NOVEMBER

Main question for staff meeting:

❋ Does our school have a culture of literacy?

Activity: Meet with the entire staff to explain what a culture of literacy is. (Refer to Chapter 1 for supporting information.) Then ask the staff to break into grade-level teams to reflect on what they're doing to promote literate behavior in their classrooms and at their grade levels. Invite each team to share what its teachers are doing with the rest of the staff. Next, bring the entire staff together to discuss and brainstorm ideas to promote a school literacy culture. Guiding questions for this discussion might include the following:

❋ What is our theme this year?

❋ How can we connect the theme to community events?

❋ What kinds of opportunities can we provide for students to interact between grades (e.g., eighth graders reading to kindergartners)?

* What activities or "days" can we host to encourage an interest in books (e.g., Dress Up Like Your Favorite Character Day, read to the local weatherman, or other special guest day)?

* What community resources do we have to help us?

* How are we connected with our local public library?

* Can we get someone from the public library to come to our school and issue library cards during parent night or open house?

* What kinds of reading contests can we promote (e.g., the grade that reads the most gets to put the principal in the dunk tank)?

DECEMBER

Main questions for staff meeting:

* How literate is our staff?

* What do we read personally and professionally?

Activity: December is a wonderful opportunity to engage the staff in self-reflective discussions about literacy for two reasons: 1) they're tired and ready for holiday break, and personal literacy is a less stressful topic than test scores or classroom reading strategies and 2) holiday break is a perfect time for the staff to read a book that you've given them.

Consider using your professional development funds to purchase two books for each of your staff to read over the holiday break, one for pleasure and one for professional growth. Give out the books at the staff meeting and tell your faculty that you'll be hosting a book talk in January to discuss one book and another talk in February to discuss the other book. Selections for book talks can be books that you think are relevant to your community or a new children's book that has caught your eye. In addition to passing out the books, engage your staff in a discussion about how you as a group can learn who reads and who doesn't. Ask your staff to discuss why they do or do not read, and explore why they think some people read and some do not. Also invite your staff to start reading professional articles found in journals such as *Kappan* or *The Reading Teacher*. Purchase subscriptions to these journals, and let teachers know where they can find them on campus (the teacher's lounge, bookroom, or professional development section in your school's library).

JANUARY

Main question for staff meeting:

* What are we doing to promote a successful standardized test experience for our students?

Activity: In some parts of the United States, standardized testing takes place during the spring semester. In other regions, testing takes place during the fall semester. Therefore, you should adjust the timing of this in-service idea to fit your school's testing calendar. Consider asking your literacy committee to seek articles and books that cover successful standardized test-taking strategies. For instance, the Association for Supervision and Curriculum Development (www.ascd.org) is a strong resource for information in this area. Also, when Autumn was a principal, she had success in increasing her school's test scores by engaging her staff in a series of book talks and strategy sessions centered on Lucy Calkins' work. Have your leadership team devise a calendar of events geared toward preparing students for the standardized tests that include practice with reading and answering test questions. Analyzing test questions and other test-taking strategies are helpful skills that will support students through a lifetime of learning.

FEBRUARY

Main question for staff meeting:

❋ What are we doing to support gifted readers?

Activity: The approach for this in-service is similar to what was outlined for October, except the focus is on gifted readers. Reread Chapter 5 to find a framework of ideas to present to your staff. Meet with each grade level individually, along with your reading specialist, to discuss test scores and how teachers have identified gifted readers. Ask your grade-level teams to be able to present information on how they've identified and supported gifted readers at the meeting. After their presentations, engage the teachers in a discussion with your reading specialist about strategies the entire team will use to engage and support gifted readers.

You can also augment these individual team meetings with a staff meeting designed to let your teachers share successful classroom strategies with each other. Like the activity mentioned in October for struggling readers, this activity is designed around a series of round-table discussions and presentations. After everyone has attended all the round table presentations, bring the entire staff back into a large group to discuss what they learned.

MARCH

Main question for staff meeting:

❋ What does a really effective literacy classroom look like?

Activity: Ask your district office administrator in charge of curriculum to identify the five best reading teachers in your school district. Invite those teachers to attend a staff meeting at your school and to be part of a panel discussion about what works in the classroom and what doesn't. Explain to your staff that the panel consists only of teachers outside your school because you want to get the perspective of those who aren't as closely involved with your community. It's very important that you clarify this point so your staff doesn't think you perceive a shortage of excellence on their part. Ask panel members to describe their community in terms of challenges and assets, and then let them share particularly successful strategies. Also ask them to share which professional development activities they've found particularly valuable.

APRIL

Main questions for staff meeting:

* How can we keep our students reading over the upcoming summer vacation to avoid summer reading loss?

* How are we utilizing our community resources?

Activity: Start your preparation for this in-service by reading Chapter 9. Look for ideas in that chapter to share with your teachers. Before the meeting, brainstorm possible ideas and programs to keep students reading over the summer. Consult with the school literacy committee. Talk with fellow school principals about what they've done to promote summer reading. Think about how community resources can be used, especially to promote summer reading. Make a list of existing and potential community partners.

To open the meeting, present your questions and what you've done in preparation to the staff. Next, divide your staff into groups, and ask them to brainstorm a list of actions and programs for summer reading and community resources that go beyond your own thinking.

Challenge staff members to think outside the box. Ask them to consider the particular attributes their spouses, family members, and neighbors have that might be employed as possible resources for summer reading and beyond. For example, Mrs. Smith's husband may be a local administrator for American Express Corporation, who might be interested in an Internet pen pal program between your fourth graders and their collections department. Mrs. Kennedy, the school secretary, may be the cousin of the owner of a local restaurant supply company who can donate snacks for students during a read-a-thon.

Also have your staff brainstorm a list of good candidates for "Principal for a Day" as a way to get people involved in your school. Perhaps Vince Bavaqua, the local TV anchorman, would be a good choice to invite to your school's Read Across America Day. After staff members create their lists, divide them into different teams and ask them to brainstorm another list of what they feel the school needs in terms of a community partnership. Then bring the entire staff back together to compare the lists of what you need and who could be contacted. Once the staff members have made those connections, have them devise a plan that includes who to contact and for what purpose. Don't forget to include a timeline that is realistic and ways to evaluate the success of the program.

MAY

Questions for staff meeting:

* What was successful this year?

* What should we focus on next year?

Activity: This is a time to celebrate. Your teachers are tired, your kids are tired, and the reality is that everyone (maybe even you) is looking forward to the close of the school year. Nothing helps morale for students and teachers like recognition for a job well done. Many schools observe the practice of end-of-the-year assemblies to recognize student achievement of some sort.

If this happens in your school, make sure that literacy activities are included—and don't forget the importance of recognizing all students' work. There are those who argue cogently that too much rewarding of behavior leads to inappropriate expectations on the part of students (Kohn, 1999). This topic is another good one for your staff to explore in terms of how you motivate students to read. Your staff could use Alfie Kohn's book, *Punished by Rewards: The Trouble with Gold Stars, Incentive Plans, A's, Praise, and Other Bribes* as a springboard for discussions about the culture of motivation in your school. You may want to order copies of this book for your staff and ask them to read it over the summer in preparation for an August retreat, or you may read it yourself and outline its main points in a meeting with your leadership team. Motivation for reading and rewarding effort are two great topics worth exploring as you reflect and prepare for the coming school year.

JUNE

Question for staff meeting:

* What are you doing to grow professionally over the summer?

Activity: The sensitive principal knows that the first answer to this question may well be "rest." The sensitive principal also understands that disconnecting from school is essential not only for teachers but also for the administrative staff as well. However, somewhere in the recognition of the importance of recharging one's professional batteries, you might consider a meeting in which you and your staff think about planning for the following school year. June is the time for teachers to celebrate the end of the year and the beginning of a vacation, while principals think mainly about hiring and master scheduling for the next year. A good strategy is to find a way to gather your leadership team for a summer planning session to talk about what the following year should look like in terms of staff development, challenges, and accomplishments from an organizational perspective. A good time to do this is usually a week after the last day of school. That way, teachers have some time to switch their mindsets from daily activities to the more global issues that long-range planning requires. Autumn knows from experience that some principals have to find funds to pay their teachers for a planning day over the summer. If this is the case in your school, plan ahead for how you'll procure those funds for such a staff development workshop.

Another opportunity for staff development could be at the last meeting of the year where you coordinate a recognition luncheon for your staff. You might share an issue that you think has possibilities for the following year's theme, or you could invite the staff to brainstorm with you what next year's theme should be. You could also invite your staff to bring a favorite book they read over the past year and make a book exchange part of the luncheon's activities. In terms of the literary "diet," the books don't have to be focused on school—they could be beach reading. The point is that you are, once again, promoting the idea that reading is important.

In addition to the above-mentioned summer planning workshop and end-of-year book luncheon, our last recommendation is that you distribute a survey that your staff can take anonymously. Ask staff members to consider what they saw as successes and challenges at your school during the academic year. Many principals also earn trust and respect by asking the staff to give them honest feedback about how they could improve as their leader. This is a courageous effort for principals, but it can reap huge dividends in terms of honest dialogue and building trust. The key for you is to focus on the patterns of responses and to address concerns that arise from the input your staff gives you. Examples of questions you might put on an anonymous survey include the following:

 * What were the great successes of your year?

 * What were the greatest challenges?

* In which areas did you feel most supported by administration?

* When did you feel the least supported by the administration?

* What can I do to help you feel more successful in the classroom?

* What would you like to see our staff focus on in terms of literacy next year?

JULY

Question for staff meeting:

* How can our staff help new teachers socialize to our school and understand what we value in terms of literacy?

Activity: July is typically the quietest month for principals. The school is a quiet, except for the few die-hard teachers who show up to chit-chat in your office. July is the month for you to finish up last-minute details before you take your own vacation—and you *should* take a vacation. You cannot be at your full potential for your staff if you haven't rested. So the question posed for this month could very easily be addressed in May or June; however, it must be addressed by July. Mentoring both the teachers new to your staff and new to the profession is absolutely essential. Check to see if you have a staff handbook. If you do, now is the time to update it. If you don't, now is the time to create one. In your handbook, include the following:

* Map of school site and teachers' rooms

* Bell schedule including lunch dismissal times and recess times

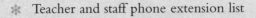

- ✳ Teacher and staff phone extension list

- ✳ Directions for how to call for a substitute if one is going to be absent

- ✳ Emergency procedures including lockdown and fire drill

- ✳ Outline of what makes a good lesson plan (see Chapter 4)

- ✳ List of community partners

- ✳ List of committees and leadership teams and their members

- ✳ A "great book" list of books you think are relevant to your school's culture

- ✳ A brief outline of what you think an effective classroom looks like (see Chapter 3)

- ✳ District calendar of holidays and in-service days

Also use July to think about your mentoring program for new teachers. Are the mentors really mentoring? How are the mentors chosen? How are they trained? Finally, how are the mentors matched with the teachers? If you're uncertain about the answers to these questions, we recommend browsing through the Association for Supervision and Curriculum Development Web site (www.ascd.org) for articles and useful information on this topic.

In closing, when you take time off to celebrate another successful year of leadership, find a book to enjoy that has nothing to do with administration, test scores, or even literacy and learning. Find one that amuses you, challenges you to think, or even takes you to a different time and place. As you know, reading will help you to escape, recharge, and keep your perspective balanced. You'll be a more balanced (and therefore, we think, happier) principal when you indulge your interests in things outside your profession. By including those books that amuse and delight in your literacy diet, you live the very thing that you want the children at your school to understand: A commitment to lifelong reading is a good thing.

Summary

Finding professional development models that best support your school's vision for literacy is one of the greatest challenges of the principalship. This task becomes even more daunting when we consider that implementation of a program is just as important as selection of a program. When these processes are done correctly, they are time-consuming and require a level of focus and commitment that is difficult to maintain because of the other demands of school leadership. Although this chapter doesn't profess to offer all the answers, we hope the chapter's insights will help you become better organized and more able to avoid the pitfalls that come with leading a new literacy program.

CHAPTER 8

What Do You Need to Know About Building Family Literacy Partnerships?

Matt Padak and his friend Chris were beginning first graders. It was raining so they were playing together in the Padaks' family room. After a bit, it got pretty quiet so Nancy went to check up on them. She found them huddled together in a corner, baseball cards strewn about, pens in hand, and surrounded by papers filled with squiggles. "What are you doing?" she asked. "Well," said Matt, "we're practicing." "Practicing?" Nancy queried. "Yes," said Matt. "We're working on our autographs for when we're in the big leagues."

Think about the ways literacy is used outside of school. Perhaps a parent and child read a storybook before bedtime. Children may write lists of hoped-for gifts at birthday time. Maybe family members look in the newspaper or on the Internet to find times for a movie or sports scores or the weather report for the next day. Children may write letters or, increasingly, e-mail messages to out-of-town relatives. Perhaps a trip to the zoo or the beach leads to an interest in birds or turtles, which leads to a search for information about them on http://kids.yahoo.com or at the public library. Family picnics or holiday dinners might conclude with family members sharing the stories that make up their family history. We could go on, but you get the point—literacy activities are alive and well outside of school as well as within school walls.

These activities are important in families' lives, to be sure, but they are also a critical ingredient in efforts to promote children's growth as readers and writers. You may recall our description in Chapter 2 of Dolores Durkin's (1966) study of children who learned to read without being taught, seemingly because they interacted in homes where both they and literacy were valued. You may also recall that Durkin followed these young readers into school and found that their early reading advantage over their peers did not disappear. In fact, it increased! Other studies of school-age children have led to similar conclusions. Parents reading to or with their children for as little as five to ten minutes per day can have an enormous impact on children's development as readers (Padak & Rasinski, 2003, 2004a, 2004b, 2005; Topping, 1987). Parents and families have considerable influence over children's reading. The evidence is too compelling to ignore. In this chapter, we focus on the critical role of parents in promoting their children's literacy growth both at home and in school.

What is family literacy?

Family literacy activities can be informal, spontaneous, and natural like many of the activities mentioned at the beginning of this chapter. These types of activities often reflect a family's ethnic, racial, and cultural heritage. Family literacy activities can also be more schoollike, as in a teacher's request that family members read together each evening. Both types—the natural and the schoollike—are important in fostering children's literacy growth.

A first important step in fostering family involvement in children's literacy achievement, then, is to help members of the school community see value in parental involvement in children's education, particularly in the non-schoollike interactions that are a normal and natural part of family life in most households. Questions like the following (Morrow & Paratore, 1993, pp. 199-200) are useful for framing a conversation about family literacy:

* How can we make family literacy a priority in our school?

* What are the components of quality home-school partnership programs?

* How can educators be confident that they are providing families with beneficial, rather than intrusive, activities?

* How can schools provide programs that take into account the needs of families from diverse cultural backgrounds who possess different literacies from the schoollike activities we are familiar with?

* How can program effectiveness best be assessed, documented, collected, and shared?

* What kinds of outcomes should we expect as a result of our family literacy programs?

Experience has taught us that effective family involvement programs are based, first and foremost, on authentic partnerships between parents and school personnel. These partnerships cannot form unless each group sees value in the contributions of the other group.

What does research say about the importance of family literacy?

Reading more often leads to reading better. Moreover, children who come to school with rich literacy experiences typically have an advantage over their peers who have not had such preschool experiences. Both of these assertions, long accepted as givens in the literacy community, speak to the importance of engaging children in reading outside of school. Yet the unfortunate truth is that many children don't read very much outside of school. The home can help here. Parental involvement in reading is an untapped source for increasing the sheer amount that students read, which, in turn, will increase their proficiency in reading.

The research is very clear on this point: Parental involvement can significantly influence children's learning in general and reading achievement in particular (Padak & Rasinski, 2003). Ann Henderson (1988; Henderson & Berla, 1994), for example, concluded that parent involvement leads to improvements in grades, test scores, and overall academic performance. Results from nearly every National Assessment of Educational Progress have found an achievement advantage for students who are regularly involved with their families in literacy-related activities. Similarly, an international study of reading instruction found that the "degree of parental cooperation" was the most potent of 56 significant characteristics of schools most successful in teaching reading (Postlethwaite & Ross, 1992).

Experimental research results also point to the value of parental involvement in children's reading. Children whose parents engage them in family literacy activities have accelerated oral language development (Senechal, LeFevre, & Thomas, 1998), greater phonemic awareness and decoding ability (Burgess, 1999; Purcell-Gates, 1996), and higher overall reading achievement (Cooter, Marrin, & Mills-House, 1999; Foertsch, 1992; Morrow & Young, 1997) compared to their peers without such opportunities. These studies, as well as dozens of others (see Padak & Rasinski, 2003), tell us convincingly that efforts to form partnerships with family members are well worth our time and school-wide attention.

How can you increase parental involvement at home?

Unfortunately, ongoing and consistent efforts to involve parents in children's reading have proven difficult to sustain. Many teachers we know have described unsuccessful and unrewarding experiences when working with parents. Some teachers feel they don't have the time or energy for such a program when they seldom get release time, remuneration, or recognition for it. Most parent-involvement programs in reading tend to be one-shot affairs such as talks by local experts in reading, "make it and take it" workshops, a note sent home urging parents to check homework or read to their children, or short-term incentive programs. These approaches have little effect on students' reading achievement or attitudes, particularly those children who struggle with reading (Padak, Sapin, & Baycich, 2002).

Creating and sustaining an effective home-school partnership requires something different, and fortunately, research can help you here. Successful programs to involve parents in their children's reading share several attributes (Padak & Rasinski, 2004a, 2004b). These characteristics can become the guidelines that school personnel use in designing their own programs to meet specific needs. The following guidelines also can be useful for diagnosing an existing program that isn't working as effectively as it might.

USE PROVEN AND EFFECTIVE STRATEGIES

We all lead busy lives, and most parents are no different in this regard. Since parents may have limited time to devote to working with their children, at-home activities must be based on proven, appropriate, and successful methods. Too often, this hasn't been the case. For instance, some at-home activities have questionable value for improving literacy achievement. Coloring pictures, cutting out photographs from magazines, or completing worksheets may not be the best use of parents' and children's time together at home. Later in this chapter we describe several much better alternatives.

PROVIDE TRAINING, COMMUNICATION, AND SUPPORT

Most parents aren't teachers. They need good and understandable training that includes demonstrations and opportunities for discussion and questions. Someone who is enthusiastic about and committed to parent involvement should provide the training. This may be a teacher, the library/media specialist, or a parent volunteer. Continuing communication and support can provide parents with timely feedback about their questions and concerns and can encourage persistence. For example, an ongoing column in the school newsletter can focus on the at-home program. Monthly sessions at school, either formal parent workshops or informal "coffee conversations," also can prove useful. Even something as simple as offers of personal contact by phone or e-mail can encourage parents to persist with their at-home literacy activities. Ongoing communication and support build bonds between home and school and demonstrate to parents that other people care about their children's literacy growth.

A very simple yet effective at-home literacy activity is for parents (or some other more advanced reader) to read to their children. This is true for children of any age. Reading aloud to children provides them with a model of fluent reading and offers parents natural opportunities to discuss the texts or for young children to point out text features such as words, letters, and so forth. Parents and children reading together (chorally) and parents listening to children read are also excellent opportunities to foster children's reading growth. These simple activities—read to, read with, and listen to children—are powerful ways to promote student growth in reading, and they form the backbone of successful at-home literacy programs.

Texts for these activities should be authentic (e.g., nursery rhymes or other simple poems, song lyrics, jokes, jump-rope rhymes for young children; all or parts of fiction and nonfiction picture books, more advanced poems, or speeches for older children). Children should be able to read the texts successfully with enough support from parents. Lots of excellent children's poetry is available in children's poetry anthologies and at the following Web sites:

* http://ucalgary.ca/~dkbrown/storsong.html

* http://www.veeceet.com

* http://www.poetry4kids.com

PROVIDE TEXTS

Some home reading plans fail because parents lack appropriate texts or the time or resources to acquire them. Certainly, we want to encourage regular trips to the public library but requiring them as a condition of participation in at-home reading activities might discourage parental involvement. The easiest solution is to provide parents and children with reading materials. When the materials are provided, parents are more likely to do the activities with their children since the materials themselves act as reminders. Our recommendation is that school personnel select texts for at-home reading programs and send them home with children. The small amount of time and money invested in doing this will pay rich rewards in broader and more consistent parental involvement.

MAKE ACTIVITIES EASY, CONSISTENT, AND ENJOYABLE

Parents tell us they're frustrated by activities that are too complex, take inordinate amounts of time, or change from day to day or week to week. They say it's hard to develop a routine of working with their children under these conditions. We think that these reactions are understandable and that at-home reading activities need to avoid these problems. At-home activities should be relatively brief (ten to fifteen minutes several times each week), simple routines with some variation to keep interest high. Predictable, time-efficient, high-interest routines increase the likelihood that the at-home activities will be conducted regularly and successfully.

Consistency is important as well. Once an effective instructional routine is introduced, a family should avoid major changes or disruptions in it. A family should be able to develop a level of comfort with the routines. Variety can be introduced by changing the texts and the ways in which parents and children respond to what they read.

If everyone enjoys the activities, persistence is more likely. A sense of informality and playfulness infused into the activities can help achieve this goal. Parents should be reminded to be enthusiastic, provide positive encouragement, and support their children's attempts to read. Allowing children some control over activities also lends enjoyment to the sessions. If the reading is followed by some word games, for example, children can choose the games as well as the words to include.

PROVIDE WAYS TO DOCUMENT AT-HOME ACTIVITIES

Documenting at-home activities allows us to evaluate the program's success in achieving its goal. More importantly, perhaps, documentation gives parents tacit encouragement and reminds them to continue working with their children. Parents can use a log sheet to record the work with their children over a specified period of time. Parents tell us that posting the sheet in a prominent place reminds them to take time for at-home reading.

Periodically, the log sheets can be returned to school where teachers, other school staff, or parent volunteers can tally involvement.

Increasing parental involvement in children's reading is somewhat time-consuming and might even be called challenging, but the potential payoff is quite high for children. As we've pointed out, research is very clear on this issue. We believe that many parental involvement programs fail either because they don't adhere to the guidelines presented above or because single teachers attempt to organize all aspects of the program by themselves.

Parental involvement should be a school-wide activity. Although the particulars of parent-child interactions may differ according to children's ages and reading ability, all members of the school staff can join in making parental involvement a priority, planning parent training and support activities, logging family involvement, and planning occasional celebrations to keep everyone motivated. Sharing responsibilities in this way increases the likelihood of success and also fosters positive school-community relationships.

What are some research-based at-home activities?

Because of the guidelines explained above, and also because educators are now more than ever challenged to articulate the research-based reasons for doing what they do, we should know that the at-home activities we undertake make a difference for children. The three programs described below, Fast Start, Reading Millionaires, and Paired Reading, have proven effective in fostering children's reading achievement. Moreover, evaluation data about both Fast Start and Reading Millionaires show that children enjoy the routines and develop positive feelings about themselves as readers.

FAST START

Fast Start (Padak & Rasinski, 2004b, 2005) is an at-home program we developed at Kent State University for parents or other caregivers and their young (K–2) or struggling readers. Parents read short, highly predictable texts with their children and then play developmentally appropriate word games in a 15-minute routine. Teachers provide the texts, which children take home weekly, and also indicate the level of word play that is appropriate for the child. The three following levels of word play have proved successful:

* Concepts about print, such as counting lines or words, finding letters, saying beginning letters

* Phonemic awareness, such as playing rhyming games, "stretching" words by saying them very slowly and asking the child to tell what the word is

* Beginning reading, such as sorting words by vowel sounds, playing sight vocabulary games ("Go Fish," "Concentration")

The Fast Start routine begins with the parent reading the text to the child, after which they read it chorally, perhaps several times. Eventually, when the child is able to read the text independently, the parent invites this and provides support, encouragement, and praise. Then the parent and child play word games for a few minutes.

Research into Fast Start (Padak & Rasinski, 2004a, 2004b; Rasinski, 1995; Stevenson, 2001) has shown it to be very effective and, as important, very enjoyable for parents and children. For example, a two-year study in 18 elementary schools showed that kindergarten children who participated in Fast Start learned letters and concepts about print faster and developed more extensive writing vocabularies than children who didn't participate. Moreover, first-grade children who participated in Fast Start outperformed their non-Fast Start peers on published tests of reading achievement. An astonishing 91% of children in these studies said they enjoyed Fast Start, and 98% said they thought Fast Start made them better readers. Their parents agreed: 83% believed that the Fast Start sessions with their children represented time well spent. It's clear that this relatively simple routine has power to affect children's achievement as readers.

READING MILLIONAIRES

Reading Millionaires is a school-wide program with a single goal: one million minutes of independent reading over a specified period of time such as a school year. Its achievement results have been impressive (Baumann, 1995; O'Masta & Wolf, 1991; Shanahan, Wojciechowski, & Rubik, 1998). As importantly, it sends a signal to everyone—children, parents, and teachers—that independent reading is a school-wide goal.

Before launching Reading Millionaires, you may want to do some initial planning. For example, decide on what will count as out-of-school reading. We recommend that you count reading to children as accumulated minutes as well as the time children spend reading silently or aloud to another family member (or pet or stuffed animal). You also may want to think about how children will report the minutes they have read. A simple calendar that includes the child's name and the teacher's name should suffice. You'll also want to decide when children will submit their accumulated minutes and who will tally all the minutes that children have read. Groups of older students sometimes do this as a school service, or parent volunteers can tally minutes read. Tallies can be kept by class on a spreadsheet. Total minutes also should be posted prominently in the school where all can see. Some schools post their total minutes on message boards on the school lawn. Other schools we know even announce which class has read the most minutes each week; Baumann (1995) created a "Reading Hall of Fame" bulletin board that featured pictures of classes of especially voracious readers. Everyone enjoys seeing the minutes add up!

Most Reading Millionaires projects begin with some sort of kick-off celebration to explain the project and motivate children and parents to participate in it. Occasional school-wide gatherings may serve to sustain interest in Reading Millionaires. Most schools have special celebrations when the school community reaches an important "minute milestone," usually a quarter million, half million, three-quarters of a million, and of course, when the million-minute goal is achieved. Many local businesses are willing to provide treats or small incentives to keep children's interest high throughout the project.

Research results about Reading Millionaires show it enhances children's reading achievement and attitudes toward reading and parents' appreciation of the importance of reading at home. A parent of two participating children wrote this after the program concluded:

> [My children] read more this year than ever before. Their interest in books was greater as were the variety of books they chose. They read more challenging books and were eager to discuss the stories and the authors who wrote them. They became so well versed in a topic that I felt I was learning from them. Please continue this program…. (Shanahan et al., 1998, p. 96)

PAIRED READING

In Paired Reading (Topping 1987, 1995), parents and children sit side-by-side and read aloud together. The child chooses the book, and the reading rate is one comfortable for the child. The parent reads in a moderately loud voice at a pace that tends to pull the child along. Either the parent or the child points to words as they are read. If the child feels confident enough to read alone, he or she signals the parent, who stops reading aloud but may whisper-read at a rate that slightly trails the child's voice. The parent continues to follow along to provide help, should the child need it. If the child stumbles, the reading together begins again. The Paired Reading routine takes about five to ten minutes each day.

In England, where Paired Reading was first developed, research shows that participation leads to significant gains in children's reading achievement—three to five times more growth in word recognition and comprehension than children had previously achieved (Topping, 1987). Moreover, because parents and children read connected text, it's logical to assume that children's fluency will improve as well.

Any of these programs, alone or in combination, can become your parent-involvement program. You might want to use Reading Millionaires as a school-wide program, Fast Start for young readers, and Paired Reading for older struggling readers, for example. Of course, the minutes children accumulate in Fast Start or Paired Reading could count toward the million-minute goal. Whatever the array of programs, the goal of fostering parents' at-home involvement in their children's literacy growth is a critical one.

How can you increase parental involvement at school?

Most schools have parent-teacher organizations to foster positive relationships, raise funds, and so forth. Yet most schools can benefit from more parental involvement. The suggestions that follow are intended to help you and your staff plan for in-school parent volunteers.

* Establish a supportive school environment. For any parent-involvement program to be successful, volunteer parents must feel welcome, comfortable, and appreciated in the school. A teacher who serves as volunteer coordinator can help ensure that parents know how helpful their assistance is. This volunteer coordinator can assist in other aspects of the program as well.

* Determine beforehand how parent volunteers can help in the school. Individual teachers may want to suggest ways for parents to work in the classroom. Such activities as reading aloud to a child, listening to the child read, or playing simple sound/word games with children can provide much-needed extra support and attention, especially for children who struggle in

reading. Fast Start and Paired Reading are as effective in-school routines as they are at home.

You also may want to use school-wide volunteers. Parents might help in the school library or media center or provide leadership for the Reading Millionaires program. A simple chart of opportunities can be useful for informing parents of the possibilities: tasks, times—remember to offer options; some parents may be unavailable during the day or for large periods of time—and who to contact for additional information.

* Provide initial training and ongoing support. This is as important for in-school programs as it is for at-home programs. For parents to be effective in their volunteer roles, they need to know both what to do and who to contact if they need help.

* Plan recognition activities. Students and staff should show appreciation for parent volunteers both formally and informally throughout the year.

These guidelines can help you and your staff plan and implement effective parent volunteer programs for your school. These programs, in turn, can support students' reading efforts in productive and satisfying ways.

How can you work with undereducated and ELL parents?

Teachers need to be sensitive to barriers that may impede parent-child reading activities. Some parents may feel uncomfortable reading aloud to their children because of their own real or perceived lack of reading ability. Parents of English Language Learners may not be fluent readers of English themselves. Parents whose own educational experiences were negative may hesitate to attend school functions. Yet all these parents want to help their children succeed. The challenge, then, is to find meaningful ways for all families to be involved in home reading activities.

To help these families, we make the suggestions below, which are based on the three research-based routines (Fast Start, Reading Millionaires, Paired Reading) described earlier. Many of these ideas, either as they are or with slight modifications, also are effective with other at-home activities.

* Seek assistance from adult educators and ELL teachers or tutors. These professionals may have specific knowledge about families' literacy levels. Even if they don't, they'll have good suggestions about the ways in which you can involve undereducated or ELL parents in children's at-home literacy activities. Share the specifics of your at-home programs with these teachers. If parents are involved in adult education or ELL classes themselves, they can learn to read Fast Start or Paired Reading texts in their own classes so that they'll be prepared to work effectively with their children.

* Ask a classroom volunteer to record children's texts for Fast Start or Paired Reading on audiotape. If possible, two versions of the text are ideal, one very slow and deliberate and the other a more fluent rendition. Children can take these tapes and inexpensive tape recorders home along with the paper copies of the texts they are to practice. The Fast Start or Paired Reading routine can be modified to begin with the parent and child reading the text while listening to the tape. They can do this several times and then proceed with the rest of the routine.

✳ Explain Reading Millionaires in terms parents can understand. Consider having explanations for at-home activities translated into languages spoken by ELL families. Help parents see that their roles in this activity are to encourage children's reading, monitor the number of minutes read, and celebrate successes.

Summary

Parents can be valuable assets in promoting children's reading growth, both in and out of school. Parental-involvement programs take some initial thought and planning. Fortunately, the most successful programs tend to be rather simple to plan and implement, and the guidelines we presented in this chapter should help you do this well.

CHAPTER 9

How Can You Build and Enhance Community, Governmental, and Media Partnerships?

It really does take a village.

In the previous chapter, we discussed the most important partnership that can exist in schools—the partnership between schools and the families whose children attend the schools. Research clearly has demonstrated the link between parental involvement in schools and students' achievement in reading and the other subject areas. Schools, however, do not exist in an isolated environment. They exist in and for the purpose of serving their communities. Over a century ago, John Dewey bemoaned the fact that schools had created artificial barriers between themselves and the communities that they served. As a result, students received an education that had little relevance to the larger life that existed outside the school walls. Since Dewey's time, schools have tried to make connections to their communities in a variety of ways.

We concur with the assessment that schools work best when they are integrally connected with their communities. We also feel that communities are better places to live when they make connections with their schools. In this chapter we explore how you, as the school principal, can foster connections between your school and the outside community to foster the literacy development of your students.

What is a community?

Let's begin by defining the community in which your school is situated. On the surface, we can say that the community is the people and organizations that exist in the area around a particular school or that have the ability to influence the life of the school. For the sake of this chapter, we've divided this notion of community into manageable chunks. You can connect with the following distinct segments of your community for the benefit of literacy.

GOVERNMENT

A number of government agencies and organizations exist in your community—some are directly connected to your school; others are not. Your state department of education and the intermediate education agencies exist to guide and support your school. Intermediate agencies, in particular, provide services such as special education and psychological support, professional development, materials, and grant-development support, to name just a few.

Other governmental and quasi-governmental agencies supported by public funding can be tapped to make your school a better place for literacy. These agencies include your city or town government resources such as the parks and recreation department, community zoo, county cooperative extension services, community library, police and fire departments, child and family services, adult basic education programs, and more.

VOLUNTEER COMMUNITY ORGANIZATIONS

Service clubs such as the Rotary and Lions clubs, the American Legion, and the Veterans of Foreign Wars can provide wonderful support to particular programs you may wish to develop in your school. Religious groups also, regardless of denomination, can fill literacy education needs that might otherwise go unfilled.

COLLEGES AND UNIVERSITIES

Most public schools are located near public and private colleges and universities. These institutions of higher learning offer a myriad of services and resources that your school can take advantage of. This is particularly true if the college has a teacher-training program; there are a large number of students and many faculty members who have a vested interest in working with the schools. Colleges also can provide a number of other resources to aid your school beyond literacy. Specialists in the arts and sciences often look for opportunities to provide service to schools in their areas.

PROFESSIONAL LITERACY ORGANIZATIONS

These organizations exist to make available a varied array of services and programs to schools around the country. In particular, the International Reading Association (IRA) and the National Council of Teachers of English (NCTE) are organizations whose membership is made up largely of teachers, scholars, parents, and others who have an abiding interest in students' literacy development. The aim of these organizations is improving literacy instruction. Thus, they can offer wonderful assistance in developing and implementing professional development programs for your faculty and other members of the school community.

These organizations also have state and local affiliates that can more directly assist and impact the literacy improvement for your school. They can help fund and otherwise support the innovative programs envisioned by the school and individual teachers.

For more information, you can visit these organizations' Web sites:

* International Reading Association (www.reading.org)

* National Council of Teachers of English (www.ncte.org)

BUSINESSES

Every community is filled with businesses that exist for monetary profit. These businesses also recognize that their future depends on connecting with the communities they serve. They often take pains to connect with local schools; the students who populate the schools and their parents represent a significant portion of their customer base. Mutually supportive relationships between schools and businesses are a natural fit.

Certain human service businesses such as elder-care facilities offer unique opportunities for your students to connect with people they might not normally interact with. Often these interactions center on literacy or use literacy as a means for making and enhancing personal connections.

FOUNDATIONS AND CHARITABLE ORGANIZATIONS

A number of foundations and charitable organizations at local, state, and national levels support educational causes. Become aware of and knowledgeable about these foundations, their purposes, and how to gain their support. They can have a major impact on your literacy program.

As you can see, a community has a wide array of organizations that can provide aid and service in literacy education to your school and its students. However, before you take advantage of these organizations, you need a plan of action for involving and using these resources.

How can your school make connections to the community?

In this section, we explore ways in which you can foster the connections to the various segments of your community so that the literacy education of your students can achieve Dewey's ideal of making education a community process. Many resources are available, but they work best if they are part of a larger coherent plan. The initial step in making connections to the community is to work with a group of interested faculty, parents, and other community members to develop a plan of action for employing community resources in your school's literacy program. The work of this committee should include the following actions:

* Inventory the resources in the community that your school might tap.

* As part of your school's larger literacy plan, develop a plan for employing community resources. Just what does the committee believe that community resources can do for the school and for individual teachers and students? These resources may range from individuals from within the community tutoring students in need, to donating money and materials to the school, to providing space in the community for displaying and honoring student work.

   The possibilities for community involvement are nearly endless. The challenge, however, is to use community resources wisely. They must be part of a coherent literacy plan in which the community resources work synergistically to maximize the effectiveness of the various resources.

* The next step is establishing communication with community resources. This, of course, requires establishing initial contact and laying the groundwork and parameters for the community involvement. The agreement to work with a community organization or business should be formalized in writing and should specify who is to be involved. Moreover, it should specify the time considerations of the involvement–the days and times in which the involvement is to occur (if appropriate) and the duration of the agreement. The agreement also should indicate the responsible parties for the school and for the community resource and outline methods of contacting each one.

* A means for evaluating success also should be part of the work of the committee. You'll need to make a plan to assess whether the partnership between your school and the community resource is actually beneficial to your school and its students.

* Access to community resources is often provided free of charge. The agency providing the service rarely benefits monetarily from its involvement. Your committee should consider beforehand ways in which the school can recognize and reward the work of the community organizations. This may mean a party or celebration for community participants, but it also could be a story or letter of thanks published in the local newspaper or a simple recognition in the school newsletter or on the school information sign.

How do you make community partnerships a viable part of your literacy program?

Is it possible to make community partnerships a viable part of your school literacy program? The answer, of course, is yes. The problem is that no one model works for all schools. Partnerships need to be tailored according to the needs of your school, the capacity and resources available in the community in general, and the needs and interests of the individual community organizations that you endeavor to build partnerships with. In this section, we describe examples of successful community partnerships that have nurtured the literacy development of students and made significant contributions to their learning in other ways and to the community in general.

CONNECTING TO ANOTHER GENERATION

In a middle school near Columbus, Ohio, the school faculty and administration forged a partnership with a home for the elderly located within close proximity of the school (Rasinski, 1988). For one semester, students enrolled in English and social studies classes were bussed to the home and partnered with individual residents of the home. The stated goal of the program was to help students develop relationships with people they might not normally associate with, learn about their lives, and learn about the aging process. The residents of the home took on the responsibility of educating their young charges in these areas of the curriculum. Literacy played an essential role in this program.

During their three-times weekly visits, students engaged in a variety of activities with their elder partners including developing personal relationships via dialogue journals; taking an oral history of the elder partner; and communicating with their elder partner through letters, poems, shared readings, and other forms of language experiences. During days that students didn't meet with their partners, they learned about the aging process by meeting with the professional staff of the home and by engaging in a wide variety of independent reading and group discussions.

The groups of students met regularly with their partners over the course of a semester. With a new semester, a new group of students began the process of developing friendships and community with their elder partners. The results of the program went well beyond the results envisioned by the project developers. For example, through the oral history project, students learned about living in the Great Depression and what it was like to leave home because the family could no longer support you. In addition, through readings and presentations, students learned what it was like to live through the uncertainties of the Second World War and the Korean War. Most importantly, students developed deep and enduring friendships with their elder partners. Indeed, in some cases, these students made it through high school and college and continued to correspond with their elder hosts.

CONNECTING TO BUSINESSES

In other schools in which we've worked, partnerships around literacy have developed between the schools and community organizations. In one case, the school connected with a local bank that had several branches within the confines of the school attendance area. Students in various art classes were invited to put their artistic efforts on public display; several pieces actually sold to community residents. Additionally, students wrote descriptions and explanations of their work for others.

Three years ago, the store manager of a local supermarket learned of the need for volunteer tutors at the elementary school near his store. He contacted the school principal, and their initial conversation led to the development of an educational partnership between the store and the school. The store manager arranged for several volunteer employees to be released from work for 75 minutes three times a week to work in the school. Each volunteer had an assigned station in the school–a quiet hallway, a corner of the school library, and especially, a room dedicated to parents and community helpers.

The school had designed a reading assistance program that these volunteers implemented. The program was based on Keith Topping's (1988) paired reading—a simple and easy-to-implement reading activity where tutor and child read aloud the same text for a short period of time, which we discussed in Chapter 8. During each volunteer's time in the school, four children visited him or her in 15-minute increments. Each student brought a book or other text that he or she was reading, sat next to the adult tutor, and, after a few welcoming remarks, began reading with the tutor for 10 to 12 minutes. After a brief discussion, the student returned to his or her classroom, and a new student began working with the volunteer. Each volunteer worked with the same four children on every visit. That effort resulted in 30 additional minutes of intense contextual reading each week for these 32 students, most of whom were struggling readers. Also, many students made substantial progress in reading, with some more than doubling the previous progress that Topping reported in his research on paired reading. The school obviously benefited from the additional instruction that the students received. The supermarket benefited from the goodwill and free advertising that came through contact with potential customers at the school and through school publications. The partnership has since grown to the point where the supermarket provides material and monetary assistance to the school and highlights and displays the achievements of the school and its students in the store. The store is a favorite destination for field trips, and store employees often will talk with students about the work they do there. The school continues to tell the story of its partnership to members of the community.

CONNECTING TO COMMUNITY SERVICE ORGANIZATIONS

Nearly every community has several service organizations that have a long history of supporting educational causes. The American Legion, for example, has been a long-time national sponsor of government education programs for high school students.

A local veterans' organization wanted to become more involved and contacted an elementary school to see how it and its members could support the school, its teachers, and its students. A dialogue began between a school committee made up of the principal and interested teachers and the leadership of the veteran's organization. The decision was made to start the partnership in a limited manner. Teachers were made aware of the veteran's organization and what it might offer. The veterans thought they could speak to students on topics and themes such as 20th-century American history, patriotism, and serving America through military service. Individual teachers invited veterans to speak to their classes.

The veterans who participated in the program apparently enjoyed the experience, for they were soon exploring ways to expand their service to the school. Teachers and veterans began looking into using veterans as buddy readers for individual students and reading to groups of students at selected times during the week.

Some teachers brainstormed ways to say thank you to the veterans for their service to the school and to the country. This came to life near the end of May in a special program put on by two classes of fifth graders. Veterans from several organizations, including some that hadn't been involved in the school partnership, were invited to the school for an evening performance. The performance included singing patriotic songs; performing historic speeches from American history, including segments of the Gettysburg Address and General Douglas MacArthur's "Duty Honor Country" speech; presenting several short readers theater presentations on patriotic themes, and ending with a choral rendering of "In Flanders Field." Several of the older veterans were moved to tears by the students' performance. A short period of refreshment and conversation among students, teachers, and veterans brought the night to an end. That performance spurred other veterans groups in the area and other schools to explore ways to support each other. The original partnership continued to blossom into the following year.

Similar partnerships can be developed with other service and philanthropic organizations such as Lions Clubs and Rotary International. Religious groups also can be partners in connecting schools to the communities they serve.

CONNECTING TO FOUNDATIONS

Several philanthropic foundations work at the national level to support large- and small-scale educational causes and projects. However, in several cities around the country, local educational foundations have been established to serve education specifically at the local level. Many act as a central receiving point for businesses and individuals who don't have expertise on school needs but who still wish to make monetary contributions to local schools. The foundations are staffed by educational experts who learn of school needs and distribute the funds according to need.

These foundations fund large- and small-scale projects to enhance students' learning and a school's success. If your school literacy committee identifies a specific literacy need to address or a literacy program to implement, foundations of this sort, as well as other private foundations, can provide the financial jump start to fill the need or make the program a reality. They can help fund and otherwise support the innovative programs envisioned by the school and individual teachers. Usually, such foundations require a short application that describes the plan and a detailed budget that shows how the money will be used.

As principal, become aware of the various foundations in your community, state, or across the nation that can provide this assistance. The school district business manager or other personnel in the central office should be able to provide you with a list of local and state foundations that may be able to support your school literacy program. In many of the schools in which we've worked, principals have guided teachers in identifying sources of funding to expand their classroom libraries. We know that improvement in reading achievement and motivation requires access to a large and varied supply of reading materials. We recommend that, at a minimum, a classroom library should be stocked with 25 books per student, not counting textbooks or other instructional type books, so a classroom of 20 students should have at least 500 books available for students. That many books is beyond the financial reach of many teachers, especially those who are just beginning their careers. Certainly, monetary support to build a classroom library is a welcome and appropriate goal for most teachers, and educational foundations can provide this kind of support.

In our own experience, principals have identified foundations that support teachers in expanding their classroom library for students. They have learned about the application process for such grants and communicated this information to their staff. In most cases, the teachers have to develop a proposal as part of the application in which they identify why they need foundational support and how they will use it. For building their classroom libraries, teachers had to identify some of the themes around which they would purchase reading materials and some of the specific titles they intended to purchase. In developing this part of the proposal, the teachers relied on other community support. First, they consulted with the Children's Choices and Teachers' Choices booklists from the International Reading Association to find recently published materials of highest literary quality that would most likely fuel the interest of their students. They also consulted with the local community bookstores to find other titles; ordering information; and tips on displaying, storing, and using the books with students. As a result of doing their homework and putting together high quality applications, five of the five teachers in the school who applied for the grant received one thousand dollars to improve their classroom libraries!

CONNECTING TO OTHER SCHOOLS

So far, we've discussed how schools can connect with agencies and organizations in their community around literacy. What we have yet to mention is that schools themselves are members of the community. You need to think about how your school might be able to connect with other schools–schools similar in nature to your school and schools that are markedly different in nature or composition from your school. Wonderful literacy possibilities arise when you think of connecting your school with other schools.

For instance, do you have other elementary schools in your local area? Think about how your school might join with other schools representing the same grade levels to promote reading. Pen pal clubs between students at similar grade levels are an obvious connection. Think about the possibility of joint literacy/service projects with students from both schools. Field trip experiences involving students from one school visiting the other school provide wonderful fodder for writing activities and projects that come from the experience. Writing done by students in one school can become the reading material for students in the other.

Is there a middle school near your elementary building? If so, a wealth of literacy possibilities present themselves. Students from the middle school are natural reading buddies and reading tutors for students in the elementary building. Research has demonstrated that cross-age tutoring and reading experiences can have a dramatic and positive impact not only on the younger students but also on the students acting as the reading buddies and tutors. In addition to direct tutoring with younger students, older students can act as literacy aides in classrooms and school libraries, too. They also can serve as powerful models of engaged reading for younger students as well as enthusiastic audiences for the younger students' reading. Older students often crave the thrill and responsibility that comes with working with younger students, and younger students are equally thrilled with the opportunity to work with students they often look up to.

School-to-school partnerships are natural ways to develop students' achievement and enthusiasm for reading. Often, all it takes is a phone call from one principal to another to get the conversation going and the partnership blossoming.

CHANGING THE COMMUNITY

We've presented approaches for the community, its agencies, businesses, and organizations to help serve the literacy needs of your students and teachers. This is perhaps the most common and fruitful direction of community partnerships—the community serving the school, but certainly the relationship can be turned around: Students can use literacy to serve the community. We've seen hints of this in some of the programs we discussed earlier. When students paired up with residents of a retirement home, they received much from the residents, but they were giving also. When veterans began working in a local school, students reciprocated by honoring the veterans with a patriotic performance.

Literacy is a tool for learning, but it's also a tool for service. Great things can happen when students begin to put their literacy tools to work in service of their communities. One of the finest examples of this school-serving-the-community-through-literacy comes from Canada where a fourth-grade teacher and his students actually changed their government and their community (Farough, 1994). The teacher, Mr. Farough, wrote that, "It was time for my students to pack up their knowledge, skills, and strategies and leave the safe but artificial confines of our public school and go after the world" (p. 627).

When his students learned about a problem in their community, they used literacy to solve it. Mr. Farough shared the problem of the illegal trophy hunting of animals in their province with his students. The students learned more about the problem by requesting in writing information about trophy animal hunting from the Ministry of Natural Resources. They studied the problem in depth through viewing film strips and videos; reading the laws, magazines, and newspaper articles; and listening to presentations by hunters' associations. They debated the issue in class with students arguing for or against trophy hunting. They learned about persuasive writing and business letters when they wrote letters to the Ministry of Natural Resources. Then, after some persuading, the minister agreed to meet the class in person.

> In courteous but persuasive words my students presented their arguments. They pinned him with their questions. He stumbled over words, shot anxious looks at me, and finding no comfort, continued on. To his credit he answered their questions seriously. He treated them like the informed individuals they were. At the end of the hour, he had promised action. He would stiffen the enforcement of trophy hunting laws and would check into providing each hunter with an education program.... On his way out, Mr. Smith touched my shoulder. He whispered, "Never have I been so passionately and so critically examined, and by 10-year-old children!" (p. 629)

This teacher and his students had indeed changed their community for the better—and they used reading and writing as their instruments. On his bulletin board, Mr. Farough has a banner that gives him great satisfaction. It reads: *We Can Make a Difference.*

This is the story of a teacher, not a principal, but we're certain that there was a principal who stood behind this teacher and encouraged him and his students to get involved in the community. As a principal, you need to give your faculty and your students permission not only to connect to the community but also to endeavor to make the community a better place. Good citizens must take on this responsibility, even if they are students in an elementary or middle school.

Mr. Farough's undertaking with his students was a large project that took time, effort, and resources. Literacy-related projects aimed at community building don't have to be so large. Students should be encouraged to do research into and learn about the problems facing their communities. Encourage them to write letters to the editor of their newspapers, write to their government leaders and representatives, and communicate in writing to other community leaders. Students can use literacy to make life easier for others by writing to the elderly and ill who live in nursing homes, reading to and with others who may no longer be able to read, putting on performances that involve reading to groups who would enjoy and appreciate their efforts, and writing to local members of the military living far from home. The possibilities are endless. When students learn that they have a responsibility to their communities and its members, and when they learn that literacy is one way to serve their communities, they will more likely become actively involved in reading and writing for real purposes.

THE SCHOOL MIRRORING THE COMMUNITY

The community can serve the school; as we discussed, in its ideal sense, the school can and should serve its community. Again, John Dewey noted that the school itself should become a community, a place where students learn to care for one another in much the same way that a community exists to be of service to its members. To that end, then, a principal can play a vital role in making the school a living and breathing community. Literacy can be of service here as well.

With your staff, think of the essential elements and roles of a community. These may include items such as the needs for safety, communication, commercial activity, education, recreation, and the need for a common purpose and financing for that common purpose.

You may wish to emulate these roles and elements in your own school. For example, isn't it possible for your school to emulate some of these functions of a community? Could students in your school run a newspaper or a book publishing company? Could your students set up a safety patrol? Is there value in developing a tutoring program in which older students work regularly with younger students, especially those experiencing difficulty in learning to read? Could students raise money to develop green spaces in and around their school building? Could you encourage students to develop commercial organizations that offer services to other students or the school community? One example is a classroom where the teacher helped students develop a recycling business that kept litter off the streets, improved the environment, and made the school a little bit of money along the way.

In Closing

The Ideal—School as an Integral Part of the Community—Make It Happen!

Schools are for learning. Schools are for serving students and others. There is no reason why these two goals have to be mutually exclusive. As a principal, you have a responsibility to help teachers and students see that the school is an integral part of their community and not separate from it. You need to help your teachers and students understand that by making the connection with the community, allowing the community to serve your school, encouraging your school to serve the community, and helping the school itself to become a community—and using literacy to make this happen—you can help your school live up to some of the highest ideals of life in a participatory democracy.

Bibliography

Adams, M. (1990). *Beginning to read: Thinking and learning about print.* Cambridge, MA: MIT Press.

Allington, R. (2000). *What really matters for struggling readers.* New York: Longman.

Allington, R. (2002). What I've learned about effective reading instruction. *Phi Delta Kappan, 83,* 740-747.

Allington, R., & Walmsley, S. (Eds.). (1995). *No quick fix: Rethinking literacy programs in America's elementary schools.* New York: Teachers College Press.

Applebee, A. N. (1978). *The child's concept of story: Ages two to seventeen.* Chicago: University of Chicago Press.

Baker, L., Afflerbach, P., & Reinking, D. (Eds.). (1996). *Developing engaged readers in home and school communities.* Mahwah, NJ: Erlbaum.

Baumann, N. (1995). Reading millionaires—It works! *The Reading Teacher, 53,* 38-51.

Bear, D., Invernizzi, M., Templeton, S., & Johnston, F. (2000). *Words their way* (2nd ed.). Englewood Cliffs, NJ: Prentice Hall.

Berliner, D., & Biddle, B. (1995). *The manufactured crisis.* New York: Addison Wesley.

Betts, E. A. (1946). *Foundations of reading instruction.* New York: American Book.

Burgess, S. (1999). The influence of speech perception, oral language ability, the home literacy environment, and prereading knowledge on the growth of phonological sensitivity: A 1-year longitudinal study. *Reading Research Quarterly, 34,* 400-402.

Christensen, R. (1991). Education for judgment. *Harvard Business School Press,* p. 99.

Cooter, R., Marrin, P., & Mills-House, E. (1999). Family and community involvement: The bedrock of reading success. *The Reading Teacher, 52,* 891–896.

Cunningham, P., Hall, D., & Defee, M. (1998). Nonability grouped, multilevel reading instruction: Eight years later. *The Reading Teacher, 51,* 652–664.

Dowhower, S. (1994). Repeated reading revisited: Research into practice. *Reading and Writing Quarterly, 10,* 343–358.

Durkin, D. (1966). *Children who read early*. New York: Teachers College Press.

Farough, D. (1994). Launching ships. *The Reading Teacher, 47*, 626–630.

Foertsch, M. (1992). *Reading in and out of school: Factors influencing the literacy achievement of American students in grades 4, 8, and 12 in 1988 and 1990.* (ERIC Document Reproduction Service No. ED 341 976)

Gambrell, L. (1996). Creating classroom cultures that foster reading motivation. *The Reading Teacher, 50*, 14–25.

Hart, B., & Risley, T. (1995). *Meaningful differences in everyday experiences of young children.* Baltimore: Brookes.

Hart, B., & Risley, T. B. (2003, Spring). The early catastrophe. *American Educator*, 4–9.

Harvey, J. (1988). *The Abilene Paradox and other meditations on management.* San Francisco: Jossey-Bass.

Henderson, A. (1988). Parents are a school's best friends. *Phi Delta Kappan, 70*, 148–153.

Henderson, A., & Berla, N. (Eds.). (1994). *A new generation of evidence: The family is critical to student achievement.* Washington, DC: National Committee for Citizens in Education.

Herman, P. (1985). The effect of repeated reading on reading rate, speech pauses, and word recognition accuracy. *Reading Research Quarterly, 20*, 553–564.

Hoffman, J., Sailors, M., Duffy, G., & Beretvas, S. (2004). The effective elementary classroom literacy environment: Examining the validity of the TEX-IN3 observation system. *Journal of Literacy Research, 36*, 303–334.

Jacobson, J., Reutzel, D. R., & Hollingsworth, P. (1992). Reading instruction: Perceptions of elementary school principals. *Journal of Educational Research, 85*, 370-380.

Keene, E., & Zimmermann, S. (1997). *Mosaic of thought*. Portsmouth, NH: Heinemann.

Kohn, A. (1999). *Punished by rewards: The trouble with gold stars, incentive plans, A's, praise, and other bribes.* New York: Houghton Mifflin.

Koskinen, P., & Blum, I. (1984). Repeated oral reading and the acquisition of fluency. In J. Niles & L. Harris (Eds.), *Changing perspectives on research in reading/language processing and instruction. Thirty-third yearbook of the National Reading Conference* (pp. 183–187). Rochester, NY: National Reading Conference.

Koskinen, P., & Blum, I. (1986). Paired repeated reading: A classroom strategy for developing fluent reading. *The Reading Teacher, 40,* 70–75.

Kuhn, M., & Stahl, S. (2000). *Fluency: A review of developmental and remedial practices.* CIERA Report #2-008. Ann Arbor, MI: University of Michigan, Center for the Improvement of Early Reading Achievement.

Lance, K., Rodney, M., & Hamilton-Pennell, C. (2000). *Measuring up to standards findings: The impact of school library programs and information literacy in Pennsylvania schools.* (ERIC Document Reproduction Service No. ED 446 770)

Loughlin, C., & Ivener, B. (1987). *Literacy behaviors of kindergarten-primary children in high stimulus-level literacy environments.* Marzano, R. J. (2003). *What works in schools: Translating research into action.* Alexandria, VA: Association for Supervision and Curriculum Development.

Marzano, R., Pickering, D., & Pollock, J. (2001). *Classroom instruction that works: Research-based strategies for increasing student achievement.* Alexandria, VA: Association for Supervision and Curriculum Development.

McKenna, M., & Kear, D. (1990). Measuring attitude toward reading: A new tool for teachers. *The Reading Teacher, 43,* 626–629.

Morrow, L. (1982). Relationships between literacy programs, library corner design, and children's use of literature. *Journal of Educational Research, 75,* 339–344.

Morrow, L., & Paratore, J. (1993). Family literacy: Perspectives and practices. *The Reading Teacher, 47,* 194–200.

Morrow, L., & Young, J. (1997). A family literacy project connecting school and home: Effects on attitude, motivation, and literacy achievement. *Journal of Educational Psychology, 89,* 736–742.

National Reading Panel. (2000). *Report of the National Reading Panel: Teaching children to read. Report of the subgroups.* Washington, DC: U.S. Department of Health and Human Services, National Institutes of Health.

National Research Council. (2001). *Scientific inquiry in education.* Washington, DC: National Academy Press.

O'Masta, G., & Wolf, J. (1991). Encouraging independent reading through the reading millionaires project. *The Reading Teacher, 44,* 656–662.

Padak, N., & Rasinski, T. (2003). *Family literacy: Who benefits?* Kent, OH: Ohio Literacy Resource Center. Retrieved April 29, 2005 from http://literacy.kent.edu.

Padak, N., & Rasinski, T. (2004a). Fast Start: A promising practice for family literacy programs. *Family Literacy Forum, 3*(2), 3–9.

Padak, N., & Rasinski, T. (2004b). Fast Start: Successful literacy instruction that connects homes and schools. In J. Dugan, P. Linder, M.B. Sampson, B. Brancato, & L. Elish-Piper (Eds.), *Celebrating the power of literacy, 2004 College Reading Association Yearbook* (pp. 11–23). Logan, UT: College Reading Association.

Padak, N., & Rasinski, T. (2005). *Fast Start.* New York: Scholastic.

Padak, N., Sapin, C., & Baycich, D. (2002). *A decade of family literacy: Programs, outcomes, and the future.* Columbus, OH: ERIC Clearinghouse on Adult, Career, and Vocational Education.

Postlethwaite, T. N., & Ross, K. N. (1992). *Effective schools in reading: Implications for educational planners.* The Hague: International Association for the Evaluation of Educational Achievement.

Purcell-Gates, V. (1996). Stories, coupons, and the TV Guide: Relationships between home literacy experiences and emergent literacy. *Reading Research Quarterly, 31,* 406–428.

Pinnell, G., Pikulski, J., Wixson, K., Campbell, J., Gough, P., & Beatty, A. (1995). *Listening to children read aloud.* Washington, DC: U.S. Department of Education, Office of Educational Research and Improvement.

Postlethwaite, T., & Ross, K. (1992). *Effective schools in reading: Implications for educational planners.* The Hague: International Association for the Evaluation of Educational Achievement.

Pressley, M., Allington, R., Wharton-McDonald, R., Block, C., & Morrow, L. (2001). *Learning to read: Lessons from exemplary first grades.* New York: Guilford.

Pressley, M., Rankin, T., & Yokoi, L. (1996). A survey of instructional practices of primary teachers nominated as effective in promoting literacy. *The Elementary School Journal, 96,* 363–384.

Quindlen, A. (1998). *How reading changed my life.* New York: Ballentine Books.

Rasinski, T. V. (1995). Fast Start: A parental involvement reading program for primary grade students. In W. Linek & E. Sturtevant (Eds.), *Generations of literacy. Seventeenth yearbook of the College Reading Association* (pp. 301–312). Harrisonburg, VA: College Reading Association.

Rasinski, T., & Padak, N. (2001). *From phonics to fluency.* New York: Longman.

Rasinski, T., & Padak, N. (2004). *Effective reading strategies* (3rd ed.). Upper Saddle River, NJ: Pearson.

Rasinski, T., & Padak, N. (2005). *Fluency first!* Chicago: Wright Group.

Rasinski, T., & Padak, N. (2005). *Three-minute reading assessments.* New York: Scholastic.

Rasinski, T., Padak, N., Linek, W., & Sturtevant, E. (1994). Effects of fluency development on urban second-grade readers. *Journal of Educational Research, 87,* 158–165.

Rubin, D. L.(1986). Achieving literacy: An essay review of two national reports on reading. *Metropolitan Education,* 21, 85–96.

Samuels, S. J. (1979). The method of repeated readings. *The Reading Teacher, 32,* 403–408.

Senechal, M., LeFevre, J., & Thomas, E. (1998). Differential effects of home literacy experiences on the development of oral and written language. *Reading Research Quarterly, 33,* 96–116.

Shanahan, S., Wojciechowski, J., & Rubik, G. (1998). A celebration of reading: How our school read for one million minutes. *The Reading Teacher, 52,* 93–96.

Shanahan, T. (2000, November). *The literacy teaching framework.* Paper presented at the annual Kent State University Reading Conference, Kent, OH.

Snow, C., Barnes, W., Chandler, J., Goodman, I., & Hemphill, L. (1991). *Unfulfilled expectations: Home and school influences on literacy.* Cambridge, MA: Harvard University Press.

Snow, C., Burns, M., & Griffin, P. (1998). *Preventing reading difficulties in young children.* Washington, DC: National Academy Press.

Stahl, S. (1992). Saying the 'p' word: Nine guidelines for exemplary phonics instruction. *The Reading Teacher, 45,* 662–671.

Stahl, S., & Heubach, K. (2005). Fluency-oriented reading instruction. *Journal of Literacy Research, 37,* 25–60.

Stanovich, K. E. (1984). The interactive-compensatory model of reading: A confluence of developmental, experimental and educational psychology. *Remedial and Special Education, 5,* 11–19.

Stevenson, B. (2001). *The efficacy of the Fast Start parent tutoring program in the development of reading skills of first grade students.* Unpublished doctoral dissertation, The Ohio State University, Columbus.

Sulzby, E. (1985). Children's emergent reading of favorite storybooks: A developmental study. *Reading Research Quarterly, 20*, 458–481.

Taylor, B., Blum, I., & Logsdon, D. (1986). The development of written language awareness: Environmental aspects and program characteristics. *Reading Research Quarterly, 21,* 132–149.

Taylor, B., Pearson, P. D., Clark, S., & Walpole, S. (2000). Effective schools and accomplished teachers: Lessons about primary reading instruction in low-income schools. *The Elementary School Journal, 101*, 121–165.

Templeton, S., & Morris, D. (1999). Questions teachers ask about spelling. *Reading Research Quarterly, 34,* 102–112.

Tooms, A. (2003). Developing leadership strategies inside the politics of language diversity and change. *The Journal of Cases for the University Council for Educational Administration, 7*(1), 1–11.

Tooms, A. (2003). A field guide to surviving the principalship. *Principal, 83(2),* 25–32.

Tooms, A. (2003). Letters to Angel: A principal's experience in literacy instruction for struggling readers. *Educational Leadership, 61*(1), 82–85.

Tooms, A. (2003). The rookie's playbook: Insight and dirt for new principals. *Phi Delta Kappan, 84*(7), 530–534.

Tooms, A. (2004). A literary Rx for teachers. *Teacher to Teacher series*. Kent, OH: Ohio Literacy Resource Center.

Topping, K. (1987) Paired reading: A powerful technique for parent use. *The Reading Teacher, 40,* 608–614.

Topping, K. (1995). *Paired reading, spelling, and writing*. New York: Cassell.

Vygotsky, L. (1962). *Thought and language*. Cambridge, MA: MIT Press.

Wigfield, A., & Asher, S. (1984). Social and motivational influences on reading. In R. Barr, M. Kamil, P. Mosenthal, & P. D. Pearson (Eds.), *Handbook of reading research*, vol. 1 (pp. 423–452). New York: Longman.

Appendix 1

NATIONAL SOURCES OF LITERACY INITIATIVE GRANTS FOR SCHOOLS AND TEACHERS

Barbara Bush Foundation

http://www.barbarabushfoundation.com/2006ApplicationGuidelines.rtf

Gannett Foundation

http://www.gannettfoundation.org/

International Reading Association Gertrude Whipple Professional Development Program

www.reading.org/awards/grantsawards.html

Laura Bush Foundation for America's Libraries

http://www.laurabushfoundation.org

MBNA Foundation

http://www.mbnafoundation.org/

Prudential Foundation

751 Broad Street, 15th Floor, Newark, NJ 07102-3777, (973) 802-4791

Scholastic Book Grants

Angela Shamel, Scholastic Inc., 557 Broadway, New York, NY 10012

Starbucks Foundation

2401 Utah Avenue South S-SR-1, Suite 800, Seattle, WA 98134, (206) 318-7022

Target

http://sites.target.com/site/en/corporate/page.jsp?contentId=PRD03-001811

Appendix 2

GLOSSARY OF LITERACY TERMS

analytic phonics "A whole-to-part approach to word study in which the student is first taught a number of sight words and then relevant phonic generalizations, which are subsequently applied to other words" (p. 9).★

basal reader series or program "A collection of student texts and workbooks, teacher's manuals, and supplemental materials" (p. 18) that are commercially published and used for reading instruction. Most basals begin with pre-primer and primer levels and extend through grade 6 or 8.

big book An enlarged version of a beginning reading book; type is big enough for children to see from a distance.

bottom-up theory of reading Often thought of as a part-to-whole approach to reading, since it is theorized that readers use letter and sound cues to begin with small parts of reading and move to progressively larger parts until the end product—meaning—is developed.

Caldecott Award An award for illustrations in children's literature given annually by the American Library Association.

comprehension monitoring Keeping track of how well one is reading and applying fix-up strategies if needed.

comprehensive reading program A program, commercial, locally developed, or both, that offers effective reading instruction for all students.

conjugation "The complete set of all the inflected forms of a verb, as *sing, sings, singing, sang, sung* for the verb *to sing*" (p. 42).

consumables The portions of a basal reader series or other instructional materials (e.g., spelling books) that must be purchased annually because students write in them (consume them).

decode "To analyze spoken or graphic symbols… to ascertain their intended meaning" (p. 55). In reading, decoding usually refers to the ability to recognize a word in print.

digraph "Two letters that represent one speech sound" (p. 60), as in *these* or *boat.*

diphthong "A vowel sound produced when the tongue moves or glides from one vowel sound toward another… in the same syllable" (p. 61), as in *oil* or *boy.*

emergent literacy A notion about young children's literacy learning that has replaced former notions about "reading readiness." Emergent literacy perspectives view reading and writing development from the child's point of view; what children know about language is valued and used to develop further insights.

English Language Learner (ELL) A person whose native language (L1) is not English.

fluency The ability to read expressively and meaningfully, as well accurately and with appropriate speed.

informal reading inventory "The use of a graded series of passages of increasing difficulty to determine students' strengths, weaknesses, and strategies in word recognition and comprehension" (p. 116).

interactive theory of reading A theory of how people read that is based on the notion of compensation. The reader is said to use all levels (e.g., letters, words, sentences) and types (e.g., phonics, context) of information, with one type compensating for weaknesses in another type, if necessary.

instructional level The level of text difficulty that is challenging but not frustrating for a child and that is, therefore, appropriate for the child's reading instruction. The instructional level is usually defined by ability to recognize at least 90% of the words in a text along with at least good comprehension.

leveled books Books that are arranged and coded according to difficulty level. Books may be leveled by publishers or through procedures established by literacy scholars. Leveled books are usually used for reading instruction; sometimes they are also used for independent reading.

literacy The ability to read and write to achieve one's purposes.

literature-based program A reading program that uses children's literature (trade books) as the major reading material.

National Reading Panel A group commissioned by Congress in the late 1990s to conduct a research review about reading in order to guide the reauthorization of the Elementary and Secondary Education Act. The Panel's findings led to the current focus on phonemic awareness, phonics and decoding, fluency, vocabulary, and comprehension as five essential elements in reading instruction.

Newbery Award An award given annually by the American Library Association to honor the most distinguished book in children's literature published in the U.S. in the preceding year.

No Child Left Behind Act The common name for the 2001 reauthorization of the Elementary and Secondary Education Act.

onset Consonant(s) preceding the vowel in a syllable (e.g., /st/ in *stop*, /b/ in *bag*).

Paradox of Educational Authority The irony that principals are expected to know everything about curriculum at their schools, and yet they cannot possibly be experts in all areas. This inevitably is linked to the politically motivated practice to "fake it" in terms of what they know because admitting ignorance means relinquishing authority.

phoneme "A minimal sound unit of speech that, when contrasted with another phoneme, affects the meaning of words in a language" (p. 183), as /b/ in *bit* versus /s/ in *sit*.

phonemic awareness Awareness that sounds (phonemes) make up spoken words.

phonics A way of teaching that emphasizes the relationships between sounds and symbols.

phonics generalization A rule to explain the pronunciation of two or more sounds in a word (e.g., "When two vowels go a-walking, the first one does the talking").

phonological awareness "Awareness of the constituent sounds of words in learning to read and spell" (p. 187) in one of three ways: by syllables (e.g., /fat/), by onsets and rimes (e.g., /f/, /at/), or by phonemes (e.g., /f/, /a/, /t/).

phonology "The study of speech sounds and their functions in a language" (p. 187).

print-free home A home environment that lacks printed materials such as newspapers, magazines, books, and so on.

receptive vocabulary Words a person can understand if he or she hears or reads them.

retelling A measure of comprehension in which the student is asked to recall what he or she can from a text.

rime "The vowel and any following consonants in a syllable" (p. 221), as /op/ in *stop* and /ag/ in *bag*).

scope and sequence "A curriculum plan, usually in chart form, in which a range of instructional objectives, skills, etc., is organized according to the successive levels at which they are taught" (p. 227).

sentence strip A sentence from a text written on a strip of paper. Sentence strips are sometimes cut apart or organized to produce the original text.

sight word(s) Word(s) recognized in print automatically.

specialized reading program Program designed for use by special populations of children, such a gifted readers, ELL students, struggling readers.

synthetic phonics "A part-to-whole phonics approach in which the student learns the sounds represented by letters and letter combinations, blends these sounds to produce words, and finally identifies which phonics generalizations apply" (p. 250).

syntax The ordering of and relationship between words and other elements in a phrase or sentence. Yoda, for example, does not have proper syntax because he would say, "Went to the store I did." Rather than "I went to the store."

thematic instruction "The organization of instruction around themes or topics instead of around subject areas such as mathematics or history" (p. 256).

top-down theory of reading Often thought of as a whole-to-part theory of reading; readers are thought to hypothesize about the meaning of the text as well as individual words and then to test the hypotheses using the visual cues in the text (letters, words, pictures, graphics) as well as the meaning that develops as the text is read.

trade books Library books

whole language A philosophy of language learning, rooted in progressivism, that is based on natural language learning with authentic materials and "led" by the child.

word recognition The process of determining the pronunciation of a word in print.

word wall A bulletin board filled with words children know or are in the process of learning.

Zone of Proximal Development Somewhat akin to the instructional level in reading (see p. 216); a Vygotskian notion that describes the "distance" between what a child can do independently and what he or she can do with the help of a more advanced "other" (teacher, parent, peer).

★ The source for all page references is Harris, T., & Hodges, R. (Eds.). (1995). *The literacy dictionary: The vocabulary of reading and writing*. Newark, DE: International Reading Association.

Appendix 3

WEB SITES FOCUSED ON LITERACY ISSUES AND LEADERSHIP

www.aspa.asn.au
Australian Secondary Principals Association (ASPA) is the national association for leaders of governmental secondary schools in the eight states and territories in Australia. ASPA seeks to meet the individual and professional needs of educators. This Web site posts a report on literacy and leadership in the middle years and is the result of a project that was funded nationally under the Australian Literacy and Numeracy Programme.

http://cela.albany.edu
The Center on English Learning and Achievement (CELA) at the University of Albany in Albany, New York.

www.cenmi.org
The Center for Educational Networking is a mandated activities project of the Michigan Department of Education. The focus of information is on leading change in schools and ensuring equal opportunities for learning.

www.ciera.org
Center for the Improvement for Early Reading Achievement
http://www.cliontheweb.org/principals.html
Examines the principal's role in improving literacy

www.ed.gov/free
U.S. Department of Education: federally supported teaching and learning resources

http://www.ed.gov/parents/landing.jhtml
This Web site was created and funded by the federal government for parents who want to help their child learn to learn.

http://reading.indiana.edu
ERIC Clearinghouse on Reading, English, and Communication

www.mcrel.org

Mid-continent Research for Education and Learning

www.naesp.org

National Association of Elementary School Principals

www.nationalreadingpanel.org

National Reading Panel

www.ncrel.org

North Central Regional Educational Laboratory Center for Literacy program evaluation tool. This is a national accrediting body for high schools across the United States. The program evaluation tool can be used by staff to examine the quality of their own programs at the high school level. For feeder schools, (K-8 and middle schools), the tool is a good instrument to consider what is being done to help support eighth graders transition to their freshman year.

www.ncte.org

The Web site for The National Council of Teachers of English, a large body of elementary, middle, and high school teachers. Members also include university professors and other researchers interested in issues concerning reading and writing.

www.nifl.gov

National Institute for Literacy

www.principalspartnership.com/feature302.html

This Web site focuses on "leadership in literacy for high school principals" and discusses the reading challenges for students beginning high school.

www.reading.org

The International Reading Association is considered by many academics and practitioners (including these authors) as the premier international organization whose body of members focuses on all issues related to reading and the teaching of reading. Members include reading teachers of all grade levels, school administrators, and academics.

Index